Reading Photographs
to Write With
Meaning and Purpose

GRADES 4–12

Leigh Van Horn

INTERNATIONAL
Reading Association
800 BARKSDALE ROAD, PO BOX 8139
NEWARK, DE 19714-8139, USA
www.reading.org

The International Reading Association attempts, through its publications, to provide a forum for a wide spectrum of opinions on reading. This policy permits divergent viewpoints without implying the endorsement of the Association.

Executive Editor, Books   Corinne M. Mooney
Developmental Editor   Charlene M. Nichols
Developmental Editor   Tori Mello Bachman
Developmental Editor   Stacey Lynn Sharp
Editorial Production Manager   Shannon T. Fortner
Design and Composition Manager   Anette Schuetz

Project Editors   Stacey Lynn Sharp and Rebecca A. Fetterolf

Cover   Design, Linda Steere; Photograph, Jerry Van Horn

The publisher would appreciate notification where errors occur so that they may be corrected in subsequent printings and/or editions.

Library of Congress Cataloging-in-Publication Data

Van Horn, Leigh.
  Reading photographs to write with meaning and purpose, grades 4-12 / Leigh Van Horn.
      p. cm.
  Includes bibliographical references and index.
  ISBN-13: 978-0-87207-612-9
  1. Pictures in education--United States. 2. Visual literacy--United States. 3. Composition (Language arts)--Study and teaching--United States. 4. English language--Composition and exercises--Study and teaching--United States. I. Title.
  LB1043.67.V365 2008
  371.33'52--dc22

                                                                                          2007048986

To my husband, Jerry, and to my students at the University of Houston–Downtown—the teachers of tomorrow—for leading your lives in ways that impart learning and love.

CONTENTS

CHAPTER 4

Discovering the Community:
Reading Photographs to Write About Relevant Social Issues

CHAPTER 5

Envisioning People, Places, and Events:
Reading Photographs to Write Narratives

APPENDIX

What to Read: Featuring Photographs

INDEX

Leigh Van Horn is an associate professor of language and literacy in the Department of Urban Education at the University of Houston–Downtown in Texas, USA. Prior to joining the university, Leigh was a middle school reading teacher for students in grades 6–8. Leigh conducted a study of meaning making and empowerment with her seventh graders and wrote about it in *Creating Literacy Communities in Middle School* (2002). She has written numerous articles for professional journals, such as the *Journal of Adolescent & Adult Literacy, Language Arts, Voices From the Middle*, and *The Urban Review*, and a chapter about her research in *Critical Ethnography and Education* (2001). She is currently editing a book on middle school reading (*Reading on the Edge: Enabling, Empowering, and Engaging Middle School Readers*, in press). She served as the editor of the Professional Book Review column for *Voices From the Middle* for seven years.

Leigh came to the university to share her love for teaching with those who want to become teachers and with those who want to further develop their teaching and learning through graduate studies. Inspired by the lives of her students, their hardships, and their determination to succeed, she is continually challenged to design experiences that will honor and expand upon their ways of knowing and help them do the same for their students. Her research and teaching interests are focused on the development of critical thinking and authentic, socially relevant curriculum that will empower learners personally and academically.

Funded by a grant from individual contributors and First Books, a national nonprofit organization whose mission is to provide children from low-income families with the opportunity to read and own their first new books, Leigh is currently learning to design experiences that will build upon what families are doing to help their children become more literate by working with families who are homeless or in transition and have children under the age of 6. Together they are reading, drawing, singing, making music, and planting gardens. She is also learning that literacy events, while they won't eliminate hardship, provide us with moments of joy from which we can draw when we need strength.

> ### Author Information for Correspondence
> Please feel free to contact me with questions or comments about this book. You are welcome to e-mail me at vanhornl@uhd.edu.

For the last several years, I have been working with preservice and in-service teachers and students in urban settings developing ideas about the use of photographs as stimulus for writing and for critical media literacy. Photographs, whether they be our own family pictures, photographs of the community in which we live, pictures of participants in historical events from our social studies texts, or photographs in the magazines we read, can stop time and provide us with a way to reenvision or relive a moment. Photographs can also help us understand ourselves and others.

My interest in reading, talking, and writing about photographs began when my parents gave me a Polaroid Swinger camera for my 10th birthday. I was fascinated by the way the pictures emerged when I wiped the blank photographic paper with a somewhat smelly sponge applicator of chemicals. I took numerous pictures of my younger sister, Martha, and my pet parakeet, Sahara, writing stories about them in an old insurance calendar I used for a journal. My interest in reading, talking, and writing based upon photographs moved into the classroom when I became a middle school teacher. Here, with my students, I began to explore writing about objects of personal significance that often included photographs (Van Horn, 2001); writing about photographs of the community surrounding the middle school where I taught (Van Horn, 2002); and the development of literacy communities through reading, writing, and talking, which I wrote about in an earlier book (Van Horn, 2002). I am particularly interested in the idea of reading and writing about photographs as it relates to critical or visual literacy or to a curriculum intended to emerge from and chronicle the lives of the students and those in the community surrounding the school.

With this book I hope to provide you with a view of specific learning experiences, materials, and examples of writing that emerge from a curriculum integrated with studies of photographs. I want to invite you to incorporate these learning experiences with what you are already doing in the classroom to help your students write with specificity, voice, and passion. When we choose to bring photographs into our classrooms from the lives of our students, from the community surrounding our school, and from the world at large, we enable our students to view and interpret images and to then write from the concrete. It has been my experience that young and developing writers benefit from having the "real" in front of them as they write. In particular, their writing becomes more specific, more detailed, and more thoughtful. As writers become more thoughtful, we begin to hear more of their individual voices. As writers become more thoughtful and engaged in their writing, the questions "How long does it have to be?" and "What do you want me to write?" disappear from the classroom.

Who Should Read This Book

This book is written for preservice and inservice language and literacy teachers of grades 4 through 12 and for social studies, history, and other content area teachers who want to explore alternate ways of reading and writing about history and people. Each chapter focuses on a different genre and ways of reading and writing with photographs to enhance student thinking and writing in that particular genre. All instructional approaches presented are designed to be integrated with your already existing curriculum.

What This Book Will Include

This book includes specific examples and descriptions of how photographs can be used to inspire the writing of memoirs; to record images of things we value and the people, places, and objects that define us; to help us reconstruct the voices and lives of others; to record images and ideas about social issues in our community; and to frame a narrative. In each chapter I have included descriptions of a number of learning experiences that will scaffold student understanding of a genre of writing.

The learning experiences in each chapter are arranged in order of increasing complexity as a way to build students' understanding of a genre and provide practice writing in the style used by that genre, with the final activity being a full-length piece in a writing genre based on a photograph and using the skills used throughout the scaffolding activities. Each activity in a sequence should take students back to what they know and then forward to another level of knowing. Think of these experiences as a recursive cycle in which students are continually challenged to exercise and expand their literacy skills as they attain more knowledge about a concept.

To get started, you may choose to do a focused study of a particular type of photograph and writing genre and use all of the learning experiences described in a single chapter, or you may choose to use learning experiences that seem most appropriate for your students and try several of them from each chapter. The opening vignette and photograph that begin each chapter serve as a model for the type of "reading" that students will do in that chapter. At the beginning of each description of a learning experience, I have included a bulleted list of the individual strategies and activities that will occur during the experience. These lists should be helpful to you as you develop your plans and choose the strategies and learning experiences you want for your students.

In chapter 1, "Remembering Meaningful Moments: Reading Photographs to Write Memoirs," we begin by having students sort, categorize, and engage in meaningful conversations about personal photographs. Students will then work on developing the concept of a memoir as they read and talk about the published memoirs of others, both picture books and excerpts from full-length memoirs. As they respond to published memoirs, they will create lists of words, phrases, and images used in memoirs. Writers then create various types of memoir: list memoirs, "remember" photo collage poems, and eventually personal memoirs based upon a single photograph.

In chapter 2, "Understanding the Who and the Why: Reading Photographs to Write About Ourselves," we begin with an examination of issues of identity by examining novels and short stories in which the main characters examine their identities. Students will then examine texts that link photography and identity. Next, students will construct poems based on their names and create a photo collage representing scenes from literature. Then, students will use a variety of photographs to create a Photo-Life Map, where students will record images of the things they value and the objects, places, and people that define them. The final activity is an essay exploring identity using the analytical tools developed in the previous learning experiences.

In chapter 3, "Creating Biographies With Voice: Reading Photographs to Write About People," we begin by examining photos of others and engaging in a discussion about understanding individuals' stories and voices. We analyze and write about photographs of people and text in informational books to simulate the decision-making process of biographers and then write a dialogue poem based on this understanding. Then, students will write two different types of poems that will help further their understanding of biography writing. First, students will choose a photograph from the Library of Congress website and write a prose poem. Second, students will search for the most important facts and details in informational texts and then use this information to write and perform an Important Poem. To further develop the concept of voice, students will read excerpts from primary-source documents and then conduct an oral history interview. The final activity involves students in writing a biography about a person in the community.

In chapter 4, "Discovering the Community: Reading Photographs to Write About Relevant Social Issues," we begin by examining photographs that depict issues of social relevance. Students will read a text about a social issue and respond by writing found poems to re-create the essence of the text. Then students will make their own observations about their communities and write about problematic events or issues of concern in their journals. Finally, students will take photographs of their community to help them identify social issues and then choose one of those issues of social concern to write about.

In chapter 5, "Envisioning People, Places, and Events: Reading Photographs to Write Narratives," we begin by having students respond to visual messages through a whole-class analysis of *Zoom* (Banyai, 1995b) and *Re-Zoom* (Banyai, 1995b). Students then examine advertisements that use photographs to tell stories about people. Photographs used for advertising purposes often include compelling images of people and a setting that is used to create a feeling or a mood. The photographs portray events or attempt to make us think and feel a certain way. Students look at the denotations and connotations as they search for the hidden and not-so-hidden meanings behind the images. Then, students will analyze picture books and wordless texts that help them begin to write narratives based upon images, and in partners they will write two-voice narratives that enable them to "listen" to the views of two different people. To make further connections between visual images and narrative writing, students will choose an art reproduction and write from the point of view of one or more of the characters or subjects within a painting. Finally, students will choose several photographs or take their own photographs and work from them. They will use what they learned of image analysis and narrative writing to compose a narrative based upon photographs.

Accompanying each activity are Reflection Points where I will invite you to stop and consider your own classroom, how you might make this work for you, how this connects to what you are already doing in your classroom, or other relevant topics. These Reflection Points provide an opportunity for you to dialogue with yourself and with me before moving on. You can use them in the way that is most helpful to you—either to interrupt the reading for thought or as a final point in your reading.

Finally, in the Appendix, "What to Read: Featuring Photographs," I have included a compendium of annotated bibliographies of picture books, young adult literature, poetry books, short stories, and other works that relate to the importance of photographs and that might be used to stimulate thinking and reflection specific to the chapter topics in this book. The Appendix is structured in such a way that you can refer to the work by the chapter of the book to which it relates and by the title of the book itself. Information about each work includes a brief summary, as well as notations about genre, grade level of interest, and how the material might be used. Each text is coded to show you whether it would be best suited for teacher background information only, teacher and student read-aloud, independent reading by students, or for student research and the development of background information by students.

I hope that you and your students will find that reading and writing based upon photographs provides you with new ways of examining literacy and examining your lives. As you explore the learning experiences in this text with your students, I also hope that you will think further on what I've presented to you and create additional activities on your own. I look forward to hearing from you about what you are doing in your own classrooms as you explore literacy and writing through photography.

Acknowledgments

I would like to thank the immensely supportive and caring International Reading Association team. My greatest appreciation goes to all of them for their confidence in me and their desire to help make this the best possible book for all of you. Thanks to Corinne Mooney, Executive Editor of Books, for her encouragement as the book took shape and incorporated the ideas of the reviewers; to Stacey Sharp, Development Editor, for her tireless, thoughtful, and thorough work in making sure that everything would be clear and useful to readers; and to Production Editor Becky Fetterolf, Editorial Production Manager Shannon Fortner, and the entire Design and Composition team for creating the look of the book and bringing it out into the world.

REFERENCES

Van Horn, L. (2001). Reading and writing essays about objects of personal significance: An exploration of meaning. *Language Arts, 78,* 273–278.

Van Horn, L. (2002). *Creating literacy communities in middle school.* Norwood, MA: Christopher-Gordon.

LITERATURE CITED

Banyai, I. (1995a). *Re-Zoom.* New York: Puffin.

Banyai, I. (1995b). *Zoom.* New York: Puffin.

Reading and Writing About Photographs in Grades 4–12

HIDDEN IN A CORNER cabinet in the hallway, crinkled and fading with time, is my collection of photographs. These photographs are old friends who speak to me of the past when I have the time to listen. Tucked inside a heavy cream-colored envelope are the photographs given to me by my father-in-law when my mother-in-law, Dorothy, passed away years ago.

As I look at them I can still remember the awe and sense of responsibility I felt when he presented me with an old dress box filled with family memories: photographs; news clippings; postcards sent from "the boys" while they were in the service; birth and death announcements; a statement of charges of $45.30 to Davis Hospital in Pine Bluff, Arkansas, USA, where Dorothy gave birth to the son that I would marry. As my father-in-law and I sat together and talked about what was inside this box, I realized that I was now to be the keeper of the family memories.

As I look through the family photographs given to me by my father-in-law, I begin, without thinking, to sort them into categories: special events, ordinary days, the boys when they were little. I mentally seek and label the main ideas, the settings, and the characters or elements contained in the photographs. There are pictures taken out in the country, at indoor settings, and in town settings at the ice cream parlor or in front of the general store. There are pictures of the entire family, pictures of Dorothy with a friend, pictures of Dorothy alone. My husband transforms from a tiny boy whose leather belt is cinched so tight it laps over four or five inches past his waist to a strapping young man in a U.S. Navy uniform, eyes squinting into the sun. Then my fingers brush against a photograph of Dorothy, my mother-in-law, sitting on a quilt outdoors, having a picnic with friends.

The photograph is yellowed and fading, yet I think I may be able to recognize the quilt they sit on. Dorothy is at the right edge of the quilt. There is a man next to her, raised up on his

knees and holding a canned drink in his hand. His right arm reaches out to support a young boy standing next to him. The boy's left arm rests in the crook of the man's arm. Next to this boy is another boy who is partly obscured by a woman in a checker-patterned shirt who is turning to smile at the camera. Behind the group to the left is a wooden picnic table. Beside the table is a metal container with a lid. On the table is an assortment of boxes. In the distance I can see tree trunks and tall grass. The blanket is laid in an area where the grass has worn down to a few sparse blades coming up from the dirt. The right edge of the photograph is darker and somewhat blurred as if there were a shadow from a large tree moving into the scene.

It occurs to me that through my description of what I see I am "reading" the photograph, using words to describe the inhabitants and elements within the quarter-inch white paper border that frames it. It also occurs to me that when we look at a photograph of people we know, our interpretation or meaning making of what is depicted in that image is closely tied to events and emotions we associate with the photograph itself. Looking at this photograph of Dorothy picnicking with her friends makes me think specifically about the quilts she made like the one depicted in the photograph. During the first few years of our marriage, my husband and I hung one of these treasured quilts on the wall behind our painted iron bed. No amount of talk could convince me that Dorothy's quilts could be picnic blankets. Now I keep them carefully folded with tissue inside them in a tiny linen closet. They rest, backside out, on the third shelf, beneath the cream afghan she knitted for me and above her last red voile holiday apron in the pale blue-and-white box. These quilts define her for me; they remind me of the care she put into all that she did. They remind me of her loving hands and the talent within them. When I miss Dorothy I can wrap myself in her quilts and feel as if I am with her again. When I look at this photograph of her sitting on one of the quilts with friends, I want to talk to her and know more about this moment. Knowing that I cannot, I may imagine what I think is happening and create a "story" of the photograph.

As a teacher, you have likely noticed that your students place great value in their photographs. I notice that many of my students have photo collages inside their lockers and on their notebooks. At lunch, after they have finished eating, I see them sharing and talking about pictures from the latest school dance. Some pore over magazines, talking about clothes and people. Others come to class early to sit with friends and look at the photo albums of pictures I have made of them in class and during school events.

Are photographs important to you as well? Think about objects that matter to you for a moment. I have a china saucer filled with old buttons placed where I can see it every morning when I am getting dressed. I have a worn basket bowl filled with the mother-of-pearl insides of oyster shells in the room where I work. I have a photograph of the Gulf of Mexico that I look at when I want to relax. Several years ago when members of my community returned to our homes after evacuation due to a threatening hurricane, many of us talked about what we had brought with us in the car. In the frantic chaos of those last few minutes prior to evacuation—with dogs barking, cats hissing, and spouses and children calling to us—what objects had we thought we could not live without? Many of us brought objects whose importance might not be evident to others, objects that defined us, objects that spoke to us, or objects that gave us comfort or happiness. Many of us brought photographs.

So why are photographs so important to us? Photographs hold moments for us—moments we have lived, and moments lived by others. Photographs draw us in and take us back. They make small moments memorable, they tell us stories, and they let us tell stories. As such, photographs can also serve as a powerful inspiration for writing and literacy.

In this Introduction to *Reading Photographs to Write With Meaning and Purpose, Grades 4–12* I will begin to establish the base ideas that will be enriched in the chapters to follow. Here you can begin to think about photographs as texts. You can consider the connections between visual and written communication and how photographs serve as cultural and personal artifacts. You will begin to discover the similarities and differences between reading print and visual texts as you think about how one might go about reading a photograph. Finally, you will learn about the instructional benefits of teaching with photographs and how you might integrate photographs with your existing curriculum.

Photographs as Texts

Defining literacy and what constitutes text has become increasingly complex. Literacy encompasses much more than the ability to read and write. To help our students become literate in today's classrooms, we now reflect upon and design ways to enhance our students' ability to think, listen, speak, read, write, view, and visually represent the meanings they develop as they engage with texts. In turn, we have expanded our definition of *text* to include not only traditional print texts but also verbal, visual, and electronic texts. Texts may be defined as messages that are composed, received, and interpreted whether they are verbal or nonverbal, print or nonprint. For the purposes of this book, literacy will entail the act of making meaning with multiple texts—texts will include both print and nonprint representations, including photographs.

Photographs are texts in that they hold messages within their borders. The elements in a photograph—or the objects, people, background, and positioning of elements in the photograph—are the "words" of the text. A viewer, or "reader," of a photograph examines the elements or "words" within the frame. He or she interprets or makes meaning of the elements by considering the positioning of those elements and their relationship to one another. This "reading" of the elements or "words" is similar to the reading of print text in that the reader must actively process the text and that the reader may come away from the experience with an interpretation or meaning that is unique from that of another reader.

Our reading of print texts is often colored by our prior knowledge or our cultural perspective, and this experience is similar in our reading of photographs. Moran and Tegano (2005) explain that photographs are signifiers of meanings that may be culturally situated, saying, "Photographs have been used as artifacts that chronicle behaviors, places, and experiences, making photography a part of ethnographic methods" (p. 2). They explain that meanings will be different for different viewers depending upon their "personal life experiences, knowledge, and perspectives" (p. 3).

We might also consider paintings, films, and the illustrations in books as visual texts that impart meaning. We are surrounded by photographs and other nontraditional forms of texts every day. During a typical day I may encounter photographs on billboards during my drive to school, an abstract painting in the lobby of the school, photographs on materials from publishers that show me the covers of the latest works in language and literacy as I pick up my mail, illustrations in picture books I am using to help students develop concepts about literacy, and then I may go home and watch a film after dinner. My ability to acknowledge and interpret these images helps me expand upon my thinking. Similarly, when we engage our students with multiple forms of texts we help them expand upon their thinking. When we engage our students with multiple forms of texts we help them acknowledge and expand their definition of reading and begin to see that it is possible to "read" outside of books, magazines, newspapers, and electronic messages to the world around them.

Making meaning will include reading, writing, speaking, listening, thinking, viewing, and visually representing our understandings of texts. It will also encompass four aspects of literacy in practice, as described by Freebody and Luke (1990), wherein readers are able to (1) decode or break down texts, (2) develop understanding or meaning from text, (3) use text functionally, and (4) analyze texts critically and transform texts. My thinking about texts is based in the work of Heath (1994), who writes that "talk, as well as talk about talk, nonverbal reinforcements of spoken and written language, written artifacts, and the activities and role regulations that frame all of these become the texts that those who study language socialization attempt to study" (p. 213).

Au (1993) notes that student success is enhanced when we allow our students to learn through different modes and when we use our awareness of our students' lives and ways of knowing to help us develop culturally responsive learning experiences. As such, to bring photographs into our classrooms is to work with our students in a different mode; using visual rather than written texts. Photographs are visual texts that tell stories through the content and placement of objects and people.

Connections Between Visual and Written Communication

Mitchell (1994) writes that "all media are mixed media, and all representations are heterogeneous; there are no 'purely' visual or verbal arts..." (p. 5), supporting the idea that there are multiple forms of texts. George (2002) writes about the connections between visual communication and written communication in school, telling us,

> If we are ever to move beyond a basic and somewhat vague call for attention to "visual literacy" in the writing class, it is crucial to understand how very complicated and sophisticated is visual communication to students who have grown up in what by all accounts is an aggressively visual culture. (p. 15)

She goes on to trace the development of ideas about the connections between visual literacy and writing over the last 50 years, beginning in 1946 when consumers of the Dick and Jane reading series were taught to attend to the illustrations as sources of meaning as well as the words. Later, in 1961, the National Council of Teachers of English issued a report on television and the teaching of English, which encouraged teachers to help their students to become informed, discriminating, and creative consumers of television. Further suggestions from others included the use of television and other visual images as prompts for writing. According to George, "Visuals (be they paintings, films, comic books, or television narratives) were to be studied in the same way as literary texts, as subjects of close analysis" (p. 17). George suggests that recent thinking emphasizes the visual nature of text itself through graphic design and electronic texts.

With that in mind, we can consider the relationship of photography and writing not only as one in which photographs might be analyzed but as one in which photographs could be used to construct and indicate the meanings held by the photographer-writer. Here, we can think of the *photographer* as the one who creates the image and the *writer* as the one who "reads" and responds to the image through writing. As your students respond to photographs and engage in the activities described in this book, they will become the writers, sometimes exploring the photographs and their meanings through writing and other times reading the meanings associated with the photograph "written" by another.

Photographs as Cultural and Personal Artifacts

Photographs are texts that are produced by many individuals for many reasons. Photographs are taken to "hold" an event, a moment, a person, or a place. They represent things that we value or that we want to ponder further. As such, photographs are cultural artifacts. Moje, Dillon, and O'Brien (2000) reflect that texts are cultural tools that help individuals come to know themselves and their ways of knowing. If we agree that photographs are texts, then they too can become cultural tools or artifacts: objects that give us information about the ideas, customs, and values that are passed down from one generation to another. As we work with our students using photographs—as they categorize family pictures, reflect on objects or moments of personal relevance, and photograph and talk with people in their community—our students will come to know themselves and their ways of knowing. Through these experiences, we have a unique opportunity to work with our students to create ethnographies of their culture and understandings, actions and interactions.

Students who work with photographs they create themselves are making what we might call personal artifacts. Like cultural artifacts, these personal artifacts document ideas, customs, and values. In this case, they reflect the student's personal thoughts. These photographs may exemplify his or her life outside of school. Students need to see themselves in school. They need to feel that their thoughts and ideas are acknowledged and respected. Inviting our students to create and work with photographs that represent what is important to them enables us to acknowledge them in ways that we might not be able to do with other texts. Student writing becomes more articulated and detailed when they work with physical objects in front of them as they write. When students work with photographs that illustrate or demonstrate their personal life, values, and thoughts, they reach a deeper understanding of themselves; then what is "real" signifies not only what is physically present but what is meaningful to them as an individual.

What Does It Mean to "Read" a Photograph?

In some ways, "reading" a photograph is a similar process to the one we experience when we read any print text. As stated previously, the photographer encodes a story in the photograph, and the viewer or reader decodes that story through the lens of his or her own prior knowledge and experience. Thus, in the same way we access our background knowledge before we begin to read text, we must access our background knowledge before reading a photograph. Consequently, just as readers of print text can have differing interpretations of a piece, readers of a photograph may make meaning or develop understanding of an image differently. As described earlier, Moran and Tegano (2005) describe the relationship between photographs, photographers, and viewers as follows: photographs are signifiers of meaning, photographers encode a story in the context of a photograph, and viewers decode this story through the lens of their own subjective interpretation and context. Sturken and Cartwright (2003) have also noted that viewers of photographs decode or "read" the meaning.

Therefore, reading photographs involves three different layers of processing. The first layer is a surface-level reading in which we may identify what is there in the photograph and how it is placed. Once we have done that, we can move to the second layer; we are ready to think about the possible meanings connected to what is there (people, objects, and nature), as well as the possible meanings of the placement of the elements in the photograph (i.e., is there a reason why something is foregrounded, backgrounded, placed close to something else?). When we write based upon the photographs we "read," we move to a third layer of processing in which we reflect, refine, or even invent based upon what we have read.

In most languages, readers of unillustrated text read from left to right. However, when we first begin to read a photograph we may begin with an overview of the image as a whole and then move into the photograph. This overviewing of the image can be compared to skimming a print text or to previewing a text by looking at the titles and subtitles. Then, we will move into the photograph in various ways, depending upon the image. Some images call for us to read from the center out or from the outer edges toward the center. Other images invite a left to right or a right to left reading. Still others may organize themselves so we want to look from what is in the foreground to the background or from the background to the foreground. For example, when I read the photograph of my mother-in-law, I look at her first and then move outward to study the others on the picnic blanket and then the grounds where they are having the picnic. I look closely at how they have positioned themselves in relation to one another and the objects around them. I can begin to think about what their placement may mean as I move to the second reading of the photograph.

In the second layer of reading a photograph, we may begin to decode the story intended by the photographer and to develop our own interpretation. What is happening in and "behind" the image? What do we "see" and "not see"? When I continue to look at this particular photograph, I read that Dorothy and Therman, her husband, have gone for a drive with friends and stopped to have a picnic at a roadside park. Dorothy has dressed for the occasion in a crisp cotton dress. Therman is taking a photograph to record the occasion. I don't see any evidence of their sons, so it is possible that this photograph was taken before they had children. As I continue to read the picture, I may begin to hear sounds and dialogue. I may think further about what happens before and after the picture is taken and continue to weave a story of my own. At this point I am no longer reading the photograph itself; I am reading my interpretation of the photograph. If I were to write this story I am imagining based upon my reading and reflection, then I would be moving to the third and final layer in the process.

Therefore, we can make the connection that the reading of photographs, like the reading of print texts, will contribute to individual subjective meanings or interpretations. George (2002) cites John Berger, who writes in his book *Ways of Seeing* about a critical aspect of seeing and helps clarify the relationship between seeing and words:

> Seeing comes before words. The child looks and recognizes before it can speak. But there is another sense in which seeing comes before words. It is seeing which establishes our place in the surrounding world; we explain that world with words, but words can never undo the fact that we are surrounded by it. The relationship between what we see and what we know is never settled.... The way we see things is affected by what we know or what we believe. (pp. 22–23)

Brown (2005) cites the work of Susan Sontag, who explains that "the initial meaning and interpretation of a photograph may change as the description or environment is modified or altered and therefore, photographs by themselves cannot create meaning but need verbal or written clarification and contextualization" (p. 151). This leads us to the conclusion that a photographer chooses a subject and composes a photograph intending to convey his or her understanding of an object or an event. Then a viewer sees the photograph and interprets it through the lens of his or her own knowledge and life experiences. The same viewer may "read" the same photograph in a different way and derive a different meaning from the viewing depending upon the context of the viewing or upon the new knowledge and life experiences that have occurred since the time of the initial reading. This means that what one feels, says, or writes about a photograph can evolve with time or place.

Writing About Photographs

Within the chapters of this book, I will engage in a "dialogue" with you and demonstrate how students can use photographs as a stimulus for writing poetry, dialogue, interviews, descriptions, memoirs, biographies, narratives, investigations, histories, and summaries. Thus far, I have alluded to the power of writing with photographs, but before you delve into the chapters that follow, which describe specific writing activities and focus on specific aspects of writing, it will be helpful to formulate a foundation of ideas about how students might generally approach photograph-inspired writing.

Writer's Journals

First, consider where students will collect their thoughts and ideas about their photographs. If you and your students are not already using writer's journals in your classroom you may want to consider doing this. In general, I find that it is helpful to have students keep writer's journals where they can collect ideas about writing and where they can respond to their reading. At the beginning of the school year, I invite my students to choose what they want to use as their writer's notebooks or journals. Some purchase a spiral notebook, while others purchase a journal (see Figure 1 for an example of a writer's journal). Still others make their own book. I buy blank sketchpads with heavy spiral binding and brown paper covers to use as my own journals.

Figure 1
Example of a Writer's Journal

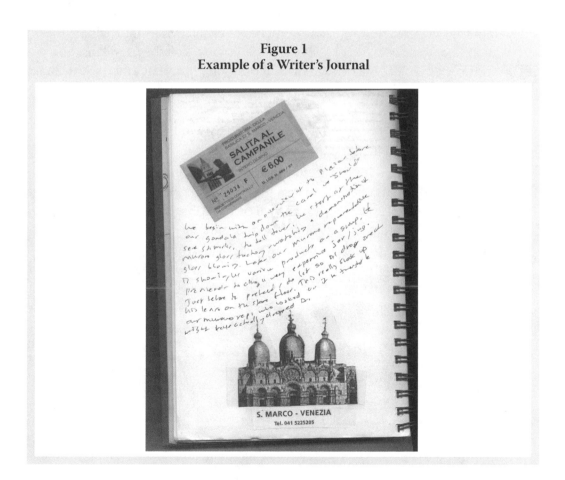

When we have our journals in hand for the first time, I talk to my students about Lucy Calkins's (1994) concept of the journal as a place where writers rehearse or remain in a state of readiness to write. Calkins writes about writers who live with a sense that they are "one who writes" (p. 23) and how this sense generates in writers an "extra-awareness" (p. 23) to the world around them. She describes a writer's notebook or journal as a "tool for rehearsal" (p. 24). Similarly, you may want to introduce some of these ideas to your students. Inform students that in their journals each artifact and the words surrounding it define them as a writer. In the pages of their journals, they can collect their thoughts and reflections and write freely, and this is where their voices can begin to grow.

Another way to introduce your students to the idea of a writer's journal is to show them your own journal. At the beginning of the semester, I pass around some of my own writer's journals and let my students examine the journals as I talk about my passion for keeping these notebooks. I tell them about my car journal for recording impressions of what I see and hear while stuck in traffic on the highway, trip journals for journeys, and everyday journals for recording the things I "read" in the world around me as I observe, think about, feel, and wonder as I experience each day. My journals are messy and filled with special rocks, sticks, photographs, sketches, napkins, and paper tea-bag labels—anything that will bring the moment and its associated impressions back to me.

Understanding Photograph-Inspired Writing

When students write using photographs, they write with a tangible item there in front of them, an item that they can study and refer to as they reflect and compose. A visual object such as a photograph enables students to have a constant frame of reference for their writing. It has been my experience in working with writers in both middle school and university settings that writing from concrete images or objects produces writing that is more focused, detailed, and elaborative than writing generated without concrete images or objects.

Naturally, the *process* of writing a piece based upon photographs will vary depending upon the genre. In the chapters to follow, you will discover how we can scaffold the experience and engage students in the process of writing in a number of genres. However, in order to provide an initial demonstration of the concept of photograph-inspired writing, we will use the genre of biography as a model.

Imagine that you want to write a biography of someone you do not know personally. Imagine that this individual is someone who is a local or national figure and someone who has been photographed and written about by others.

You might begin by collecting all of the photographs of this person that you can find: photographs of him or her alone, with others, at work, during recreation, in public and private venues, and so on. You might place these photographs on your desk or wherever you are going to write or in your writer's journal. As you "read" each photograph you will record thoughts and ideas about what is included in the photographs and perhaps what is not. You may look deeply at the individual's face and begin to formulate a detailed description based upon what you see in a single image or in multiple images.

As you continue to write, you may record ideas about the person based upon photographs that depict his or her interactions with others. You may write about what you can observe of how he or she goes about working and playing. As you revise and refine your notes, your final piece might be based solely upon the photographs. You might even weave the images into the piece to create a biography of the images and reflections and possible conclusions drawn *from* the images. You might also use what you have written about the photographs as the basis or frame for an expanded piece in which you include references to other works that have been written about the individual and excerpts from his or her own work or writings.

Instructional Benefits of Reading and Writing About Photographs

Bryant (1996) states that "we share common ground in finding that interactions with photography are crucial to our critical practice—they prompt us to read in new ways" (p. 19). I would expand this idea to say that photographs prompt us to read *and* to write in new ways. As I read Bryant's words *critical practice*, I think about how important it is for us to continually reflect on how we are engaging our students. Reflection includes reading, thinking, and talking about meaningful ways to expand the literacy experience for our students. Therefore, this section will outline the number of instructional benefits of incorporating the use of photographs with classroom instruction as a way to expand our students' literacy experiences.

Enhancing Comprehension With Photographs

Providing experiences for our students to code verbally and nonverbally as they work with photographs may be of benefit in terms of both student engagement and comprehension of texts. Hibbing and Rankin-Erickson (2003) support the idea that using photographs can aid in comprehension when they write about students' drawings, text illustrations, picture books, and movies serving as visual stimuli that help reluctant and struggling readers in middle school comprehend texts (we can reasonably include photographs, a similar visual stimulus, in this listing). They continue by describing a dual coding system as "the coding of knowledge in both verbal and nonverbal representations" and suggest that "the elements of both systems are intricately connected" in ways that "allow us to create images when we hear words and to generate names or descriptions of things we see in pictures" (p. 759). For example, we might ask our students to "illustrate" a text with photographs they take themselves, or after reading a short story, chapter book, or informational piece, students could reread and create a list of mental images in their writer's journals. Students could then take pictures that correlate with these mental images, either by locating similar settings and objects in the world around them or by creating their own still life and photographing it. These photo representations may serve as a visual retelling of the written text. Another way we might have students consider the meaning of words is to have them choose several words from a text they are reading, words from course-related vocabulary, or words they want to know more about. When students have the words in mind, they can "define" the word by composing and taking a photograph that represents the meaning of the word.

Enhancing Multiple Literacies and Knowledge of Multiple Cultures With Photographs

As we read and write about photographs in our classrooms, we can help our students examine and come to know our multiple cultures and multiple literacies. We come to know multiple cultures as we share exploration and writing we have created based upon photographs through the activities in this book: our memoirs, pieces we have written about our own identity, oral histories, interviews, biographies, pieces investigating issues of social relevance in the community, and perhaps even narratives. Each piece that we create using photographs to write with meaning and purpose provides a representation of ourselves and our cultures.

In a series of articles compiled for a themed issue devoted to "New Discoveries in Literacy for the 21st Century," Bennett (1998) notes that

> policymakers at the Educational Testing Service are basing their new assessments on the fact that in the very near future "instruction will be adapted...to personal interests and background, allowing more meaningful accommodation to diversity than was possible with earlier approaches." (p. 12)

According to Alvermann and Hagood (2000), "For students to perform well on the new assessments, they will need to develop a critical understanding of how all texts (both print and nonprint) position them as readers and viewers within different social, cultural, and historical contexts" (p. 193). As I noted in the previous paragraph, the process of reading photographs and writing about photographs provides students with an opportunity to learn about one another. As the students examine the photographs of their peers, they can "see" into alternate lives. Listening to what others have written and participating in response groups centered on discussions of the pieces provides the students with opportunities to ask questions and to delve further into their understandings of cultures and lives other than their own. Through this process our bonds as a literacy community or a community of readers, writers, and talkers is strengthened to the point where we come to look upon this time spent together as a highlight in our learning experiences.

We develop understandings and come to know multiple literacies when we infuse our literacy experiences with viewing and meaning making based on visual aspects such as photographs. As we engage our students in literacy experiences based in photographs, their understanding of literacy expands and images become powerful texts. As we work with our students in this way, we begin to develop what Wink (1997), in writing about critical pedagogy, terms *conscientization*. Wink describes conscientization as a state that enables teachers and students to "have confidence in their own knowledge, ability, and experiences...the power we have when we recognize we know that we know" (p. 26). Students who choose or create photographs and who "read" and write based upon photographs are developing alternative ways of thinking. As they grow more confident with the methodology, they become more confident in their readings and writings. Students generate meanings. Students express themselves and what they know in visual and written texts. Conscientization develops further when people who know that they know question practices and ways of doing things that do not support what they know. That is what we do as teachers when we reflect and choose experiences that help our students develop multiple literacies.

Increasing Students' Motivation to Write

As I have worked with my students, I have learned that taking photographs and writing about them in multiple ways will motivate students to write lengthier and richer pieces than ever before. Some of their enthusiasm may be based on the novelty of working with photographs. Others may be motivated as we use photographs to support our thinking and writing in a variety of genres. Some indicate that they find that the individual experiences that help us build knowledge about the genre are helpful. Others are motivated by the element of choice or the opportunity to explore their lives and the lives of others through photography, talk, and writing.

Kist (2005) describes classrooms where teachers and students are engaged in multiple ways of working with multiple texts as new literacy classrooms. Kist defines new literacy classrooms as those that "feature daily work in multiple forms of representation," invite student discussion of the "merits of using certain symbol systems in certain situations with much choice," have teachers who demonstrate the problems in working with various symbol systems, provide opportunities for students to work individually and collaboratively, and are "places of student engagement" (p. 16). I envision new literacy classrooms also as places where students exercise voice and find the power that they have within themselves, and writing activities inspired by photographs enable students to do this.

Other students who are not native speakers have noted that working with an image in front of them, whether the image is one they have created or one created by another, gives them a starting point. We begin by writing about what we see and then we think further about and explore that which is seen. Those who are working from self-created images or images that include their own experiences begin working from a visual reference to what it is they know: a moment, a feeling, or a person. In essence they own the photograph because they have lived it, and having lived it gives them the power to write about it.

It is not only their writing pieces that tell me my students are engaged; I know this because of what they tell me. Many say, "I can't have a day without writing anymore!" Others who have gone on to other grades or classes are eager to show me that they continue to keep journals, filling them with photographs, writings, drawings, cards and notes from their friends, and ideas for future writing. I knew I could state positively that my students had increased motivation to write when one of them came to class with a torn brown paper bag in her hand, exclaiming, "I was staying at a friend's house and I just had to write. I couldn't find any note paper so I wrote on this paper bag I found in the trash can."

Integrating Photographic Texts With the Existing Curriculum

Teachers in many content areas can benefit from integrating photographs with their curricula. Teachers in all content areas share a desire to enhance students' comprehension of texts, experiences with and knowledge of multiple literacies, understanding of diverse cultures, and motivation to write. Through an integration of photographs with our existing curriculum across content areas and grade levels, we can address these issues. Many content area teachers already have photographs in their textbooks and classroom materials. With some small adjustment they can engage their students in "reading" photographs to write with meaning and purpose. For example, in a social studies class students can work with a photograph chosen from a collection of images of people arriving at Ellis Island before and after a study of immigration in the United States in the early 1900s. Before reading about the period, the students could write observations about what is contained in the photograph, and after reading the writing would then center on an imaginary inner dialogue of one of the individuals in the photograph. The photographs can then be projected onto a blank wall or screen, and the writers can read aloud what they have written. This experience could be adapted to a number of topics in the social studies curriculum. Before studying a unit in science devoted to the environment, students could write about photographs of local areas of environmental concern. During the unit of study the students might visit one of these local areas and participate in clean-up or information-gathering activities. Photographs could be taken to document the process and later used as images to accompany a written commentary about the events and the knowledge gained. These are just a few examples of ways that photographic texts can be incorporated with the existing curriculum, no matter what the content area.

And, of course, photographs can enhance an English language arts curriculum. All of the activities in this book can be easily integrated with any English language arts classroom, and as you read this book and engage your students in the learning experiences with photographs, you will no doubt think of additional ways you can incorporate photographs with your existing curriculum. I have already described how students can use photographs to help them enhance their comprehension as they retell a text using images. In an English language arts class, while reading a novel students could choose a particular chapter or scene and create a collage of images cut from magazines to depict that chapter or scene. Students could then stand in order of chapters or scenes and discuss the elements of their photo collages. The discussion would exemplify the meanings and interpretations of the students and would represent the sequence of events within the work as a whole. I did this with my seventh-grade students while we were reading *Journey* by Patricia MacLachlan (1991). It was enlightening to listen to their conversations as they created their collages. Comments such as "No, that's not the way I see him in my head," "I need a picture of a hand—it's the hand that is really important in this scene," and "Oh, so that's the way it happened, that's not what I was seeing when I read that part" let me know that the students were engaged in meaning making that was clarifying and solidifying their understanding of the novel as they talked and created their collages. In another example, students who are reading and learning about mysteries might be provided with photographs of "clues," "characters," and a "setting" and asked to collaborate to write a mystery of their own. Students might use photographs or a collage of photographs to create a new cover or an advertisement for a favorite book.

These covers or advertisements could be displayed in the school library or other common areas. These are just a few examples of the practically endless possibilities, and I have confidence that you will also find new ways to use photographs to expand upon your existing curriculum.

Conclusion

With this Introduction, we can begin to reflect on and to consider photographs as elements of literacy that we might bring into our grade 4 through 12 classrooms to enhance students' writing in meaningful and purposeful ways. Most of us have had opportunities to take and examine photographs that are important to us. These photographs comprise a visual record of what we have done and perhaps what we have thought. As we reflect here, we can begin to consider how we might expand upon our common conception of photographs as a record of personal and family events and think about them as texts that we could bring into our classrooms. We can begin to think about how our students might read photographs and how they might write based on their readings of photographs. We can begin to think about what it means to "read" a photograph and how reading photographs might motivate students to comprehend, to explore culture, and to write lengthier and richer pieces. We can begin to imagine specific ways we might integrate photographs with our existing curricula.

Finn (1994), who has published more than 45 books of photographs, writes about the art of seeing, quoting the following from an introduction author William Saroyan wrote for a book of photographs by Arthur Rothstein:

> It is our nature to look and see.... The more we look the more we see, the more we want to look, and the more there is to see.... A daisy is a simple flower until you begin to really look at it. A good photograph of a daisy will impel you to start looking at a real daisy more pointedly, and from that looking at all things more pointedly. (p. 23)

When we invite our students to explore, collect, create, read, think, talk, and write about photographs we help them look at the world more "pointedly." When we use photographs to help our students write with meaning and purpose, we help expand their vision of literacy. Our students focus not only on what is there but on what *could* be there.

REFERENCES

Alvermann, D.E., & Hagood, M.C. (2000). Critical media literacy: Research, theory, and practice in "new times." *Journal of Educational Research*, *93*, 193–205.

Au, K. (1993). *Literacy instruction in multicultural settings.* Fort Worth, TX: Harcourt Brace.

Bennett, R.E. (1998). *Reinventing assessment.* Princeton, NJ: Educational Testing Service.

Brown, E.L. (2005). Using photography to explore hidden realities and raise cross-cultural sensitivity in future teachers. *The Urban Review, 37*, 149–171.

Bryant, M. (Ed.). (1996). *Photo textualities: Reading photographs and literature*. Cranbury, NJ: Associated University Presses.

Calkins, L.M. (1994). *The art of teaching writing* (New ed.). Portsmouth, NH: Heinemann.

Finn, D. (1994). *How to look at photographs*. New York: Harry N. Abrams.

Freebody, P., & Luke, A. (1990). "Literacies" programs: Debates and demands in cultural context. *Prospect, 5*, 7–16.

George, D. (2002). From analysis to design: Visual communication in the teaching of writing. *College Composition and Communication, 54*(1), 11–39.

Heath, S.B. (1994). The children of Trackton's children: Spoken and written language in social change. In R.B. Ruddell, M.R. Ruddell, & H. Singer (Eds.), *Theoretical models and processes of reading* (4th ed., pp. 208–230). Newark, DE: International Reading Association.

Hibbing, A.N., & Rankin-Erickson, J.L. (2003). A picture is worth a thousand words: Using visual images to improve comprehension for middle school struggling readers. *The Reading Teacher, 56*, 758–770.

Kist, W. (2005). *New literacies in action: Teaching and learning in multiple media*. New York: Teachers College Press.

Mitchell, W.J.T. (1994). *Picture theory: Essays on verbal and visual representation*. Chicago: University of Chicago Press.

Moje, E.B., Dillon, D.R., & O'Brien, D. (2000). Reexamining roles of learner, text, and context in secondary literacy. *Journal of Educational Research, 93*, 165–180.

Moran, M.J., & Tegano, D.W. (2005). Moving toward visual literacy: Photography as a language for teacher inquiry. *Early Childhood Research and Practice, 7*(1), 1–25.

Sturken, M., & Cartwright, L. (2003). *Practices of looking: An introduction to visual culture*. New York: Oxford University Press.

Wink, J. (1997). *Critical pedagogy: Notes from the real world*. New York: Longman.

LITERATURE CITED

MacLachlan, P. (1991). *Journey*. New York: Delacorte.

CHAPTER 1

Remembering Meaningful Moments: Reading Photographs to Write Memoirs

THIS IS A PHOTOGRAPH of me and my younger sister standing on the porch in front of the apartment house where my mother's parents live. The afternoon sun shines on the two of us and on a somewhat leggy looking plant in a

terra cotta pot on the left. The difference in our heights is accentuated by the fact that I am standing on the top step while she stands on the second. Both of us are squinting into the sun. We are wearing matching pale blue cotton dresses with tiny collars and smocked bodices. Both of us are wearing white, fold-down socks with our shoes. Of the two, I am more formally posed, holding a small bunch of gardenias in both hands. My right foot is extended in what I am sure is an attempt at one of the ballet steps I have recently learned. My sister, on the other hand, is much more natural. She smiles somewhat quizzically, looking as if she wants to say something to the person taking the photograph. She has her hands on her hips and is standing with her feet together. Her body faces to the left and she has only momentarily turned her head away from her objective. This photograph takes me back to a time when my mother's parents lived in an apartment in Houston. It was only about a 20-minute drive from where we lived.

This is my first reading of the photograph, describing what I see, noting details and positioning. Now I can take my understanding to the next level and read the photograph to uncover or decode the story inside the memory forever captured in this image. As I do this I will think about the possible feelings of everyone associated with the picture: my own, those of my sister, and those of the person taking the photograph. I will think about the moments before, during, and after the photograph and, if possible, how these moments are connected to or disconnected from other events in my life. I will consider how this photograph might represent a particular meaningful or intense moment in my life and how I might write about it to convey that to a reader.

According to Zinsser (1987), a memoir is written about a part of a person's life that "was unusually vivid or intense" or that was "framed by unique events" (p. 21). However, memoir writing involves more than simply the recitation of a list of events. Instead, the authors of memoirs explore their lives from "multiple perspectives" and compose both a "story and a reflection" (Kirby & Kirby, 2007, xii). Zinsser supports this idea when he refers to writing a memoir as "narrowing the lens, to achieve a focus that isn't possible with autobiography" in which we "move in a dutiful line from birth to fame" (p. 21). Writers of memoirs narrow the focus and critically examine the thoughts, emotions, and actions connected with an event or a series of events. They reflect on the meanings and implications associated with the events.

Writers of memoirs usually frame their stories within historical or geographical contexts. And though writers of memoirs choose to focus on a particular event or series of events from their past, and though they often write about these moments in their lives, their points of view are altered. The writers in a sense relive the past but do so with a greater knowledge of the impact the events have had upon them and with a more mature perspective or view. Because they look upon the past from the perspective of the future and look upon their younger self from the perspective of their older self, writers of memoirs often edit or alter events as they describe what they saw, felt, or made of the situation. As a result, two memoirists will write two very different pieces about the same event. The experience of writing memoirs is intense because writers are examining and writing about the pieces of their lives.

When we use photographs to stimulate the writing of memoirs, we help our students use visual cues to focus on an event or a series of events; reflect upon the meaning and implications of the thoughts, emotions, actions of the past; consider historical and geographical contexts; and edit and alter events and perspectives to frame and reframe a story. Welty (1984) ties photography to writing in general as she reviews her life as a writer in *One Writer's Beginnings*. She reflects on a time in her life when she was taking photographs in Mississippi for the Works Progress Administration, noting,

> With the accretion of years, the hundreds of photographs—life as I found it, all unposed—
> constitute a record of that desolate period; but most of what I learned for myself came

right at the time and directly out of the *taking* of the pictures. The camera is a handheld auxiliary of wanting-to-know. (p. 92)

She describes herself as a child, making frames with her fingers from which to view the world and the people in it, and later writes,

> The frame through which I viewed the world changed too, with time. Greater than the scene, I came to see, is situation. Greater than the situation is implication. Greater than all of these is a single, entire human being, who will never be confined in a frame. (p. 98)

In this chapter we will examine and reflect upon ways that we can use photographs to help our students develop concepts about and write memoirs as we do the following:

- Sort and categorize photographs
- Engage in meaningful conversations about personal photographs
- Develop a concept of memoir through reading, talking about, and making personal connections to picture-book memoirs and excerpts from full-length memoirs
- Create list memoirs based upon the writing of Sandra Cisneros (2002) in *Caramelo*
- Read what others have written based upon their personal photographs
- Create "remember" photo collage poems based upon the writing of Paul Auster (1988) to help students collect ideas and brainstorm topics for a complete memoir
- Write a complete memoir based upon a single photograph using the analytical tools developed in the previous learning experiences

ACTIVITY 1

Sorting and Categorizing Personal Photographs

Sorting and categorizing photographs is a great way to help your students begin thinking about how photographs can be used to capture and remember meaningful moments—you may recall from the opening vignette in the Introduction that I sorted photos into categories as I went through my box of family photos. You might do this early in the year or the semester to help students get to know one another while you demonstrate the possibilities related to sorting photographs.

Before you have your students sort and categorize photographs, introduce students to the process with a read-aloud of a picture book related to the topic. When I do this with my students I begin with a read-aloud of *The Red Ball*, a picture book by Joanna Yardley (1991). The story describes a little girl looking through a box of old family photographs and "following" a red ball, which appears somewhere in each picture. Short read-alouds can be used effectively to motivate interest in and activate students' prior knowledge or experiences related to a topic of study. Any picture book that refers to photographs could be used to introduce the idea of working with photographs. For a list of other possibilities, see Table 1. Further information about the books in each chapter can be found in the Appendix.

After the read-aloud and discussion, ask students to examine their own photographs and to sort them into categories that make sense to them. Invite your students to bring in a dozen or more photographs from home. (Now that you can print copies of photographs on copy paper, this activity does not put original photographs at risk.) I usually have students use their desktops as a

Table 1
Suggested Picture Books to Use for Developing a Concept of Memoir

Angelou, M. (2003). *My painted house, my friendly chicken, and me*. New York: Random House.
Cousins, L. (2004). *Smile, Maisy!* Cambridge, MA: Candlewick.
Creech, S. (2000). *Fishing in the air*. New York: Joanna Cotler Books.
Dorros, A. (1991). *Abuela*. New York: Puffin.
Gray, L.M. (1995). *My mama had a dancing heart*. Danbury, CT: Orchard Books.
Houston, G. (1992). *My great-aunt Arizona*. New York: HarperCollins.
Ketteman, H. (1998). *I remember Papa*. New York: Puffin.
MacLachlan, P. (1991). *Three names*. New York: HarperCollins.
MacLachlan, P. (1994). *All the places to love*. New York: HarperCollins.
MacLachlan, P. (1995). *What you know first*. New York: Joanna Cotler Books.
Monroe, M.A. (2007). *Turtle summer: A journal for my daughter*. Mount Pleasant, SC: Sylvan Dell.
Mora, P. (1997). *Tomás and the library lady*. New York: Knopf.
Nickens, B. (1994). *Walking the log: Memories of a southern childhood*. New York: Rizzoli.
Perkins, L.R. (2007). *Pictures from our vacation*. New York: Greenwillow.
Polacco, P. (1990). *Thunder Cake*. New York: Philomel Books.
Polacco, P. (1998). *Mrs. Mack*. New York: Philomel Books.
Polacco, P. (2001). *Betty doll*. New York: Philomel Books.
Ringgold, F. (1993). *Dinner at Aunt Connie's house*. New York: Hyperion Books for Children.
Rylant, C. (1982). *When I was young in the mountains*. New York: Dutton.
Say, A. (1993). *Grandfather's journey*. Boston: Houghton Mifflin.
Schotter, R. (2006). *Mama, I'll give you the world*. New York: Schwartz & Wade Books.
Soto, G. (1997). *Snapshots from the wedding*. New York: Putnam.
Stewart, S. (1997). *The gardener*. New York: Farrar, Straus and Giroux.
Watts, J.H. (1997). *Keepers*. New York: Lee & Low.
Williams, V.B. (1982). *A chair for my mother*. New York: Mulberry Books.
Yardley, J. (1991). *The red ball*. New York: Harcourt Brace Jovanovich.

surface for categorizing their photographs. As they sort and create categories, ask students to write a label for the category on an index card or sticky note. Later, when students talk about these photographs and categories with their peers, they begin the process of choosing and editing the moments from their lives that they may decide to write about. As you listen to your students talk about their photographs while sorting them, you will notice they have many ideas about how they might categorize their pictures. You may hear comments like "I could sort by friends and family" or "I'm putting the pictures of my pets in one category by themselves" or "These are all pictures of me and my brothers and sisters." Once students have sorted and categorized their photos, have them create a picture portfolio to share with others, in which they will sequence pictures to tell a story. Students can sit with a partner who has placed four to six photographs on the desk in the order that he or she will talk about them. While one student talks, the other listens and asks questions to prompt the "story" about the relationship between these photographs and the unfolding of events related in the photographs. When one student has had the opportunity to talk for about 10 minutes, ask the students to reverse roles.

REFLECTION POINT

Take a handful of your loose photographs at random and arrange them on the tabletop until you begin to see different ways to organize them. Sort your photographs into columns. Using sticky notes or index cards, create a heading or category for each column. If you were to sit with someone and talk about these photographs and the way you have organized them, what would he or she learn about you? What could you learn about your students from photographs they might bring to school?

ACTIVITY 2

Photo Museums: Engaging in Meaningful Conversations About Personal Photographs

When students have finished sorting and categorizing their photographs and have sequenced the photos to tell a story, ask everyone on the left side of the room to stand up and go to visit the "photo museums" of those on the right side of the room. This provides an opportunity for students to talk about their pictures and their lives with one another. After a few minutes, have the "museum curators" exchange places with the "museum visitors." Walk around and listen to what the students are saying; take this opportunity to learn about your students and their lives outside of the classroom. When I walk around my own classrooms, I usually hear talk about family, friends, and culture; major life events; and small moments. I hear laughter and sighs. I see students smiling, showing concern, or perhaps patting someone on the shoulder before moving on. As you monitor students' interactions, you may want to note commonalities and dissimilarities in students' photographs and experiences and in the way they organize their photographs.

After they have visited each other's photo museums, have students return to the whole-class group and discuss the experience together, drawing conclusions about what has been discovered. When you ask students what they think, you will likely find that the words and ideas pour forth. Students are frequently motivated when you ask them to share what they know and care about within the classroom. When you do this you are authenticating their own experiences and showing them how their literacy and life-learning experiences outside of school relate to what they are doing in school.

As you listen to your students talk about the experience, you will find that this is an important opportunity for them to learn about one another. Most of today's classrooms are composed of diverse groups of students, and allowing them to choose and talk about photographs that reflect their lives outside the classroom provides important opportunities to build understanding and respect for differences. Further, beginning to sort ideas with photographs of their lives acknowledges and reinforces their significance as individuals.

When you help your students examine themselves and their ideas and share these thoughts with one another, you help them to know themselves in new ways as they come to know one another. As you engage in these experiences, the lives of those within your classroom are intertwined and you begin to develop a literacy community. Brandt (2001) reflects on literacy as a productive resource, stating that "literacy...is a means of production and reproduction, including a means by which legacies of human experience move from past to future and by which, for many, identities are made and sustained" (p. 6). She explains that social interaction is an originating or opening literacy experience on which to build, writing, "From a contextual perspective, literate abilities originate in social postures and social knowledge and extend well beyond the words on a page" (p. 4). When you encourage your students to talk to one another about their photographs, you are creating an originating or opening literacy experience for them.

When you use photographs as a beginning point for students to talk and then write about themselves, you are using multiple literacies to make meaning. The New London Group (2000) refers to this as developing multimodal meaning. They write that "people create and innovate by hybridizing, that is by articulating in new ways, established practices and conventions within and between different modes of meaning" (pp. 29–30). You can think of photographs and talk as two different modes of meaning making. When you ask students to sort and talk about photographs, you ask them to observe and articulate in new ways, through categorization and talk, what they know about their lives. The sorting and categorizing activity can be extended by providing students with a large sheet of paper and art tape so they can write their names and place their photographs in such a way that these photograph sorts could be displayed in the classroom. In this way your students publicize their Photo Museums where others may see them and perhaps initiate further conversation with them. My students like to see what the students in other class periods are doing. They will often gather in the room during passing periods to look at and discuss what their friends in other class periods are creating.

Many teachers teach students who may not have a collection of personal or family photographs they could bring to school. In this case, you might provide your students with disposable cameras so they could take pictures of their "outside of school" lives. You might have your students use disposable cameras to search for stories or to capture moments in their lives that they can later weave into stories. Students could store their photographs in a folio of visual images to be used as "seeds" or inspiration ideas to write about. If you have a digital camera available at your school, students might use it to take pictures in school and create an electronic folio for the same purpose. Whether students bring in pictures from home or take pictures at the school, however, these photographs could be used to stimulate further storytelling and writing.

Nobel Prize–winning novelist Toni Morrison writes of her process of thinking and discovery and its basis in the visual image and the unpacking of the image, stating, "By 'image,' of course, I don't mean 'symbol'; I simply mean 'picture' and the feelings that accompany the picture" (cited in Zinsser, 1987, p. 112). She compares the sense of discovery to that experienced by an archeologist, writing, "It's a kind of literary archeology: on the basis of some information and a little bit of guesswork you journey to a site to see what remains were left behind and to reconstruct the world that these remains imply" (cited in Zinsser, 1987, p. 112). That is the way you can envision this experience—writing based upon photographs helps us begin with something that was there and then interpret that discovery much as an archeologist would interpret the meaning of an ancient vessel or portion of a tool.

ACTIVITY 3

Close Reading of Picture Books to Help Develop a Concept of Memoir

Before asking students to write about personal photographs, you must engage them in a study of the art of writing about self: the art of the memoir. Reading and talking about memoirs and coming up with their own definitions of and ideas about memoirs will stimulate thinking about the words and pictures they might eventually use in their own memoir writing about personal photographs. Authors Rosanne Kurstedt and Maria Koutras (2000) suggest that writers look at picture books as models for writing memoirs—rather than "tell" students how to write a memoir, they ask their students in grades 4 through 8 to construct an image of what a memoir might contain as they study picture-book memoirs. Similarly, you will likely find this to be an excellent way for students to establish an understanding of what a memoir might contain and how it might be structured. Carefully chosen picture books can be used with all age groups to help introduce ideas and develop concepts about genre, including memoir. When choosing picture books to use with older readers, you will find that there is a wide selection to choose from. The picture books you will use to introduce ideas and develop concepts are not those focused on "early reading" or "how-to-read," but they are picture books that are centered on a topic related to historical fiction or human emotions and relevant sociological issues.

Begin the process by modeling your own thoughts as a reader who is trying to learn about writing through a close reading of text. Verbalize the places in the text that are important to your construction of knowledge. For example, I read aloud from the picture book *Keepers* (Watts, 1997). In this book readers learn that in Africa there is a keeper for each tribe, a female who is a "keeper of stories and legends" who "holds onto the past until she can pass it on to the next" (p. 10). I think of this individual as a "keeper of memoirs" or vivid, intense moments in the lives of people. Kenyon, a young boy, wants to be the keeper for his family, but his grandmother, Little Dolly, tells him that the honor must go to a female. As you read further, you see Kenyon talking about his grandmother with the antique dealer, the carriage driver for tourists, and the caretaker at the cemetery. Each one of them has a story to tell about Little Dolly. Kenyon decides to collect these stories and give them to his grandmother on her 90th birthday in a handmade book. You can use a picture-book memoir such as this one to illustrate how memoirs reflect important moments that you want to hold close, and moments that you want to pass down and share with others.

Collaboratively Developing a Definition of Memoir

After you and your students have read this first memoir aloud as a class, you will want to spend some time talking about what they noticed and what they can take away from the experience to help them build their concept of memoir. Invite them to share their initial ideas about what constitutes memoir. For example, students may note that memoirs can be based upon stories they may hear from others.

As you read and talk about memoirs with your students, record your ideas about memoirs and the elements of memoir in a place where everyone can see what has been shared and can add to the list as they make further discoveries. This recording place will be similar to a word wall, but it will be a wall that helps students gather and record ideas as they work to define the concept of memoir writing.

In my classrooms, my students and I jotted down the elements of memoir on large sheets of bulletin board paper mounted on the wall. These words reflected our growing understanding of the concept through the reading and discussion of texts. We could use our words to define for ourselves what we see as memoir writing. We started with the ideas we discussed after reading *Keepers*. For example, we may have written something like "memoirs are stories that we may hear from others," "memoirs reflect important moments that we want to hold close," or memoirs are about "moments that we want to pass down and share with others." One of my students, Lacy (all names are pseudonyms), expressed that memoirs are "a snippet of your life—a snapshot," so we added this phrase to our sheet. Another student, Sarita, said that memoirs are about "a magnificent piece of your life," so we added this to our sheet as well. Katlyn summed up with the words "a true story from our life—we lived it!" so we added the words "rich, rich language," and then we prepared to dig further in search of the meaning of memoir. You may want to keep notes about the book title, author, and what is said about those specific works on the sheet as well.

Then, to help writers further develop the concept of memoir, invite your students to choose a book from a selection of picture books as individuals, as partners, or in small groups (see Table 1 on page 21 for a list of suggested picture books for developing the concept of memoir). Begin by asking students to read silently to themselves and mark with sticky notes anything that they feel is helping them to develop their concept of "memoir." Then, sit in a circle and read aloud to one another, sharing what you have found.

Making Personal Connections to the Memoirs

As you remain sitting in a circle, you may want to have the students read their picture books silently a second time, this time focusing on any personal connections they might make. Then, as a class, have students discuss the personal connections they make between their own memories and the experiences in the picture books. Depending upon your students' familiarity with making personal connections to text, you may need to model making your own connections through a think-aloud of a picture book. When you make a personal connection to someone else's memoir (even if it may be an imaginary memoir, as are these picture books), you "see" something in that person's life story that reminds you of something in your own. It seems to be more natural and more effective if you allow the sharing of connections to take place spontaneously or through volunteers to an open invitation.

Experiences from my own classroom provide an illustration of this idea. When one student, Antonia, had approached the chalk rail to select a book for individual review, *Tomás and the Library Lady* (Mora, 1997) was one of the few remaining books. Therefore, it was pure happenstance that she chose this book about a family of migrant farm workers from Texas, but a few minutes into the reading I heard her exclaim softly to herself, "This is my life. The way I grew up! She is writing about me!" Antonia later read aloud to us, "Year after year they bump-bumped along in their rusty old car" (p. 2) and then told us, "Year after year we drove on those old back roads to the north. We would drive over the same old bumps and they would keep us up at night...you wouldn't believe the roads." She read aloud the words of the library lady to Tomás, "It's a hot day, come inside and have a drink of water" (p. 7) and, reminded of the heat and of water, Antonia made a further personal connection to the text, saying, "It was hot, so hot in the car, and sometimes the AC wouldn't work. We dreamed about getting out of the car. We would say to each other, 'Whenever I get out of the car this is what I'm gonna get—I'm gonna get a cold water and splash it all over my face!'" She also told the class that as she read about Tomás and his trips to the public library, it reminded her of going to a mobile home in the fields where "it was like a day-care for the kids of the migrant workers...where we could read."

As we moved around the circle, Sarita talked about how reading *Fishing in the Air* (Creech, 2000) made her think about her father. "My Daddy...Daddy never caught any fish, he baited all the hooks for us instead." Joanie reflected that reading *Dinner at Aunt Connie's House* (Ringgold, 1993) made her think of the strong women in her life. Rod told us that reading *Three Names* (MacLachlan, 1991) reminded him of the stories his mother used to tell him about her childhood in Louisiana. Chris, reading *My Great-Aunt Arizona* (Houston, 1992), told us that she grew up in a small town with a graduating class of less than 100 and said, "Reading this book about a teacher reminds me of how often I sit and think about what I'm going to be when I get older."

Talking out loud and sharing their thoughts and ideas enables readers to make personal connections and perhaps to relay a brief, similar memoir of their own. Prompted by their readings about the lives of others, students may begin to think about crucial moments in their own lives. When this occurs and students speak of these moments aloud, they are, in a sense, constructing a draft of a memoir they may write when you move them further into the experience. Record these new ideas regarding the concept of memoir on the board or on the sheet where you first recorded your students' original ideas.

REFLECTION POINT

Examine some of the picture books listed in Table 1 on page 21 and find the one you will use to demonstrate your thinking (or perhaps you may already have a picture book in mind). When you have chosen the book, develop a plan for a read-aloud in which you will model your thinking as a reader trying to learn about writing through a close reading of text. You may also want to think about personal connections you could make to this same book for a demonstration of this before students make personal connections to the memoirs they have chosen.

ACTIVITY **4**

Reading and Responding to Excerpts From Full-Length Memoirs

In the days that follow your initial experiences with personal photographs and picture-book memoirs, you will want to present your students with a selection of excerpts from full-length memoirs to help them further develop their understanding of this genre. Some excellent resources for this activity are found in Table 2, including *Barefoot Heart: Stories of a Migrant Child* by Elva Trevino Hart (1999), *This Boy's Life: A Memoir* by Tobias Wolff (1989), *Once Upon a Time When We Were Colored* by Clifton L. Taulbert (1989), and *Tales From the Homeplace: Adventures of a Texas Farm Girl* by Harriet Burandt and Shelley Dale (1997). Further information about books mentioned in this

Table 2
Suggested Full-Length Memoirs to Use for Developing a Concept of Memoir

Beals, M.P. (1995). *Warriors don't cry: A searing memoir of the battle to integrate Little Rock's Central High*. New York: Simon & Schuster.

Bitton-Jackson, L. (1999). *I have lived a thousand years: Growing up in the Holocaust*. New York: Simon & Schuster.

Burandt, H., & Dale, S. (1997). *Tales from the homeplace: Adventures of a Texas farm girl*. New York: Henry Holt.

Cleary, B. (1996). *A girl from Yamhill: A memoir*. New York: HarperCollins.

Cox, L. (2006). *Grayson*. New York: Knopf.

Curtis, C.P. (1997). *The Watsons go to Birmingham—1963*. New York: Bantam Doubleday Dell.

Frank, A. (1996). *The diary of a young girl*. New York: Random House.

Filipovic, Z. (2006). *Zlata's diary: A child's life in wartime Sarajevo*. New York: Penguin.

Greenfield, E. & Little, L.J. (1992). *Childtimes: A three-generation memoir*. New York: HarperCollins.

Hart, E.T. (1999). *Barefoot heart: Stories of a migrant child*. Tempe, AZ: Bilingual Press.

Hickam, H. (2000). *Rocket boys: A memoir*. New York: Dell Publishing.

Jiang, J.L. (1997). *Red scarf girl: A memoir of the cultural revolution*. New York: HarperCollins.

Lowry, L. (2000). *Looking back: A book of memories*. New York: Delacorte.

Myers, W.D. (2001). *Bad boy: A memoir*. New York: HarperCollins.

Osa, N. (2005). *Cuba 15*. New York: Random House.

Santiago, E. (1994). *When I was Puerto Rican*. New York: Knopf.

Taulbert, C.L. (1989). *Once upon a time when we were colored*. New York: Penguin.

Wolff, T. (1989). *This boy's life: A memoir*. New York: Grove Press.

Yep. L. (1996). *Lost garden*. New York: Simon & Schuster.

activity can be found in the Appendix. You will want to choose the excerpts from these books carefully so they are appropriate, relevant, and of interest to the students you teach. As an extension of this activity, you may want to have students in grades 8 through 12 read the entirety of a full-length memoir rather than excerpts. After a short "book talk" of each excerpt, ask students to choose the one they would like to read and think about. It may also be helpful to have students conduct Internet searches and read memoirs of people who have lived in times that are of particular interest to them. In this case, you may want to do an initial search and bookmark sites for your students. See Table 3 for some suggested websites.

Then, if you have access to enough copies of memoirs that are appropriate for your students, you can list the pages and paragraphs you want them to read and have them mark their connections and thoughts directly in the books by using sticky notes. Students might make connections between their lives and the life of the author of the memoir, between this text and others they have read, or between this text and their understanding of history or world events. Another alternative is to have your students keep a dialogue

Table 3
Suggested Memoir Websites

Migrant Farm Workers
farmworkermovement.org/essays/essays.shtml
This website contains essays by United Farm Worker volunteers from the 1960s, 1970s, and 1980s and papers from the speeches and letters of Cesar Chavez.

Women's Movement
www.cwluherstory.com/CWLUMemoir/text.html
This website includes a series of text memoirs—some reproduced from previously published material, others written from interviews or specifically for this site. An index contains brief notations about the individuals involved in the Women's Movement. Viewers of the site can listen to an audio narrative or read a written essay.

Vietnam War
www.ndqsa.com/
This website contains memoirs written about particular events and experiences of the Vietnam War. Some example memoirs are "Lost on Highway 1" by Morris Johnson and "Serving With Hawk Missiles" by Max Whittington.

Martin Luther King, Jr.
seattletimes.nwsource.com/mlk/king/speeches.html
This website contains printed and audio versions of some of Dr. King's speeches. Also included are "Letter From a Birmingham Jail" and "The Purpose of Education," an article written for a student newspaper.

journal entry of their thoughts as they read the excerpts. Many of you already have your students use writer's journals. Writer's journals are places where writers can record their thoughts, observations, ideas for writing, quotations from pieces they are reading, and other ideas about writing (see page 9 of the Introduction for more information on writer's journals)—there will be numerous opportunities for students to utilize writer's journals as they engage in the activities described in this book. Students will be able to record their ideas and developing thoughts, keep records of their thinking during a particular learning activity, list and develop ideas for writing, and so on. Dialogue journal entries are a powerful means of helping readers and writers make connections to what they are reading regardless of the text type. This is also a way to validate the life experiences of your students. As you read the memoirs of people who are similar to yourself, you begin to reexamine all the moments of your own life and to attribute greater significance to these moments. There is a feeling that you are saying, "I too have lived. I too have felt that way, and this is how it was for me."

Model for your students the types of things you want them to note in their dialogue journal entry as they read. You might start by demonstrating a place where you read something and stop to think about it. This could be noted under a heading "Things I Am Thinking." You can then pause at a place where you have read something that you want to remember for when you write your own memoir. This could be noted under a heading "Things I Want to Remember as I Write My Memoir." When you read something that reminds you of something in your own life, you can note this under a heading "Things From My Own Life That This Helped Me to Remember." To get students to attend to the place in the text that prompted these thoughts, set up the journal in four columns with the first column being "From the Text" and the other three statements heading the other three columns.

After reading, have the class sit in a circle and share their thoughts and what they have written about their readings of the excerpts from the memoirs. Two students in one of my classes, Antonia and Jen, were inspired to reflect on particular vivid and intense moments of their own lives after reading Elva Trevino Hart's description of a trip to the neighborhood store in *Barefoot Heart*. For example, Antonia wrote the following:

> I can easily take out the writer's name and place mine in the story. Her stories about what she has experienced are the same as my experiences...from the family traditions to the way she eats her popsicle and walks around barefooted, hopping from one shadow to another!

Jen, who also read the excerpt from *Barefoot Heart*, wrote the following:

> I am thinking about when Shelly (my cousin Michelle), Tia Velma, and I used to walk to the blue store—we would go barefoot. Tia Velma would buy us soda, chips, and Chinese candy with her food stamps. We always bought Big Red or Coke. Sometimes we would get pickles to put our Chinese candies in. We didn't worry about our feet getting dirty or stepping on rocks. Sometimes the cement burned, but we would jump to shaded areas.

Another student, Latresha, wrote in her journal under the title "Response to Memoir—*This Boy's Life*" a list of "words or phrases that caught me," followed by the statement "So much of his memories jogged things that I'd totally forgotten about...." Chris, another student, used sticky notes to make notations in *Tales From the Homeplace* while reflecting on memories and emotions from her own life that the text evoked (see Figure 2).

REFLECTION POINT

The books listed in Table 2 on page 29 can serve as a beginning point for you. It will be helpful to take some time to look for book-length memoirs that would be interesting to your particular students and written at a reader level appropriate for your students. Then, you can choose the excerpts you want to have your students read, mark them with sticky notes, and plan a brief "book talk" for each excerpt. Think about including books that represent the diverse backgrounds of the students you teach.

Figure 2
Chris's Notes on *Tales From the Homeplace*

What I Read (From the text)	Chris's Notes
...be sure to watch for copperheads. (p. 3)	When we would go to the creek we wore moccasins.
Mama and Daddy were barely out the door.... (p. 3)	Mom and Dad had to go to Rosenberg (closest bigger city) to get groceries.
...get out of the creek, I mean get out. (p. 4)	Country life: spend more time with siblings than friends. Drive, parents at work, friends don't live within walking distance.
...I certainly can't carry a baby and a loaded gun and watch five children with one pair of hands. (p. 5)	"snake gun" "be-be gun"
I bet Grandpa stops at the general store and buys him a soda.... (pp. 5–6)	White cotton on the side of the road after they picked and transported it. 360 Short Stop—name of our general store.
...her bare feet were frying on the dirt road. (p. 6)	What we lived on for the first three years until they asphalted it.
Don't you dare splash Annie and me.... (p. 7)	I was the oldest and always had to "watch out" or else I would get in trouble.
Suddenly she understood why some people called them mountain lions.... (p. 9)	Dad killed a large bobcat that kept attacking one of my dogs and my horse.

From Burandt, H., & Dale, S. (1997). *Tales from the homeplace: Adventures of a Texas farm girl.* New York: Henry Holt. Student work reprinted with permission.

ACTIVITY 5

Writing a List Memoir

One year while preparing to teach a course in advanced processes in writing, I discovered the book *Caramelo* by Sandra Cisneros (2002). While she does not call this book a memoir, it reads like one. One of the forms in the novel is a list of objects that are important to the person who owns them. Each object could be the focus of a memoir, or the list itself can be considered a memoir in an alternative format. For example, we read Cisneros's description of the objects in Regina's apartment in Mexico City:

> Now their apartment was packed with enough furniture to make it look like La Ciudad de Londres department store. Narcisco had to climb over brass cuspidors, musical bird-cages, obscene mirrors bigger than beds, Venetian finger bowls, crystal chandeliers, candelabras, carved platters, silver tea sets, leather-bound books.... (p. 149)

This list of objects continues for an entire page. I am sure that if Regina were a living person she would be able to tell us when and where each object came into her life, why it was significant to her, and how this object has affected her life. When you focus on a single object such as this and tell the story of the object, you are writing a memoir based upon an object or an entity. By having your students create a similar list memoir, they will learn more about how objects can prompt students to think about memorable moments—moments that can become the basis for memoirs. You may want to share this idea with your students.

Demonstrate the listing process by having your students look around the classroom with you and list everything they see that is of relevance to them. For example, together you may come up with a list like the following:

> Now our classroom is packed with the bits and pieces of all of our literate lives. Looking around you will see sheets of bulletin board paper with questions and comments about text taped to the black board, shelves stacked with our journals, files brimming with portfolios, a note board covered in sticky notes we have written to one another, quotes of our ideas about reading and writing in a border near the ceiling, foil-covered cardboard "swords" left over from our production of *Macbeth*, and historical fiction novels resting on the chalk rail with the lists of the students reading them hanging beneath, and so on.

When you have completed the list together you can choose an item from the list and collaborate to write a memoir of your collective thoughts. As an alternative, you may have students choose an item individually and jot down some of the things they would include in a memoir constructed from the moments connected to this object. For example, a shortened version of a memoir I would write about the foil-covered cardboard "swords" left over from our production of *Macbeth* would begin as follows:

> As I hold this drooping foil covered cardboard sword in my hand I can "see" Colin earnestly asking me, "How am I going to make the sword fight look real and still say my lines like I mean them?" After repeated attempts to memorize his lines, Colin devised a plan where he would write his lines in the palm of his left hand and sword fight with his right. As he slashed and jabbed with his right hand, he used his left hand as a balance, waving it in the air vehemently and then stopping to hold it out and read the lines. It wasn't entirely ineffective, and it made him feel good about his performance.

Once your students understand the listing process and how to select an item and write a short memoir about it, have them create lists of their own. You might want to ask your students to work from family photographs to create similar lists, or students could reflect on their personal spaces at home and compile a list of everything that is there. They could make a list of objects that are important to them or list moments from recollection. You might want your students to bring in actual objects or photographs of objects that they would include on their list. Again, having the real object or a photograph depicting the object helps students think deeply before and during writing.

As students create these lists, they become more observant about the spaces and objects that make up their lives. Objects and spaces that are meaningful to us are meaningful because they evoke memories of moments that are important to us. When you ask students to list what is contained in a room or a photograph, you ask them to attend to the way their lives are arranged. When you ask them to focus on a single object and write about the memories associated with that object, you help them to focus their reflections through the objects. These lists may also prompt thinking about particular moments or incidents that could later become memoirs written in a more traditional form. This list memoir is a scaffolding activity that helps students build toward writing a complete memoir. You may want to have your students choose an item and expand it into a list memoir before moving to further activities not only because it is a scaffolding activity but also because it is an interesting form of memoir in and of itself. When students have written their list memoirs you may want to have them "illustrate" the memoirs with photographs of the objects or scanned copies of the photographs used to prompt the memoir.

One of my students, Jim, creating a list memoir based on a family photograph, decided he would rather compose a list of moments that he can "see" when he looks back at the photograph, writing,

> Looking at this photograph of Rus and Travis and me in our cargo shorts and tees with our caps turned to the side and back, standing with our skim boards in our hands, ready to pull off our shirts and run at the waves. Our mothers brought us here and you can see them in the background sitting on the beach chairs we rented for the day. Beside my mom is a cooler filled with [sports drinks], peanut butter sandwiches, apples, cheese sticks, sun block, and mosquito repellent. On the chair she has a pile of beach towels, sun glasses, flip flops, books and magazines she thinks we'll read when we get tired, a radio, and her cell phone. Looking at the water and the skim boards takes me back to that moment. If I close my eyes I can hear the surf and feel myself skimming quickly and then dragging as the sand catches the bottom of my skim board.

REFLECTION POINT

Even though you are going to create a list of objects from your classroom with your students and write the list memoir based upon one of the objects as a "live" demonstration in front of your students, it is helpful to experience the process on your own before you do it with the students. Think about creating a list of objects in your home, your garden, your car, your classroom, or another place that is important to you. See if you can use one item from the list and write a list memoir.

Reading What Others Have Written About Personal Photographs

It is often helpful to students to see and hear exemplars from texts before engaging in a process. Therefore, in order to demonstrate to your students that others have written based upon personal photographs before having them write the "remember" photo collage poem in the next activity—and eventually the full memoir—you may want to read aloud excerpts from literature that refer to this process. For older students, excerpts from *Barefoot Heart: Stories of a Migrant Child* (Hart, 1999) are great for this purpose, particularly the excerpt beginning on page 52 where Hart writes, "My mother wasn't much for telling stories, but she had a shoe box full of old pictures inherited from her mother, and some of them had long stories behind them." Hart proceeds to describe several pictures and to relay the stories behind the pictures. For younger students in grades 4 through 8, you might read an expanded version of the following excerpt from *Pictures, 1918* (Ingold, 1998), which details a moment when Asia and Nick stand together in the school auditorium looking at a display of photographs gathered to encourage greater war-relief efforts.

> The pictures are stark black and white, hardly softened by gray, and they make me want to stare inside them, see *past* them…. I can almost imagine that I'm her. Maybe it's because of her eyes. How the photograph shows her eyes, and her eyes show her feelings….
>
> This is what I've been talking about, something stopped so a person can think about it. (p. 25)

You might also read from the first chapter of *Pictures of Hollis Woods* (Giff, 2002), when Hollis shows the first of many pictures (most of them pictures that she has drawn) that will encapsulate or thematically represent the intense moments of her life. In the first chapter as she holds a photograph cut from a magazine, Hollis tells readers,

> "Look for words that begin with W," my teacher…said. She was the one who marked in the X, spoiling my picture…. "This is a picture of a family, Hollis. A mother, M, a father, F,

a brother, B, a sister, S. They're standing in front of their house, H. I don't see one W word here." I opened my mouth to say: What about W for wish, or W for want.... (p. 1)

Read aloud these excerpts or pieces like them from other texts to inspire your students just before you invite them to go home to sift through their own photographs, looking at them with new eyes. Each of them will be searching for a photograph that will help them tell a special story—a memoir about an intense or vivid moment in their lives.

REFLECTION POINT

Excerpts from texts are helpful when we want to introduce our students to a variety of works and may not have the resources or time to work with the entire text. When I wanted to do this with the topic of memoir, I went to the library and checked out a number of memoirs. I then read each one and marked powerful points in the text. The excerpts are a compilation of these powerful points. Is there a topic you might develop in this way for your students?

ACTIVITY **7**

Writing About Our Own Personal Photographs: "Remember" Photo Collage Poems

You can help prepare your students to write memoirs based upon photographs with the writing of "remember" photo collage poems. A "remember" photo collage poem is actually two things: a poem of remembrances (inspired by an excerpt from a memoir written by Paul Auster) and a collage of photographs that represents the objects written about in the poem. I think of this experience as a brainstorming prelude to writing a full-length memoir. Begin with a read-aloud of an excerpt from Paul Auster's (1988) memoir *The Invention of Solitude*. Further information about this book can be found in the Appendix. In order to give you a feeling of the piece, here is an excerpt from the part that I like to read aloud:

> He remembers that he gave himself a new name, John, because all cowboys were named John, and that each time his mother addressed him by his real name he would refuse to answer her.... He remembers learning to tie his shoes.... He remembers sitting in the bathtub and pretending his knees were mountains and that white soap was an ocean liner. (pp. 166–167)

Auster remembers his father getting dressed in the morning, he remembers seeing his newborn sister come home from the hospital, he remembers thinking the world was flat, and lying in bed looking at a tree outside his window. Coincidentally, each thing that he remembers carries an image with it.

After reading, discuss the excerpt with your students. Talk about the various images called to mind by the words. Then, students may move directly to writing their own "remember" pieces, or you may even want to have your students work through the making of their first photo collage by working in small groups to create a collage illustrating the excerpt from Auster's memoir using photographs clipped from magazines. Next, invite students to write their own "remember" poems. Most of the sentences in Auster's piece begin with the words "He remembers...," and this is a great format to follow for students writing "remember" poems. I also like to have students center the lines on a page and insert line breaks so that their pieces are formatted like poems.

When students have completed their poems, they should read and reread them silently to decide what images they would need to help them create a photo collage illustrating the poem. It is helpful to have students list what they will need. Then, they may clip photographs from magazines or do as one of my students, Tenesha, did and create a photo collage using photographs she had brought in specifically for this project. With permission from parents, students may use extras or copies of photographs from home. My student Tenesha wrote the following poem:

> She remembers how she couldn't wait for school to be out for the summer.
> She remembers spending summer vacation in Jennings, Louisiana,
> with her grandmother.
> She and her cousins would play in the big ditch behind her aunt's house.
> She remembers pretending they were fishing.
> They caught a crawfish and poked it with a stick so they could watch it move.
> She remembers walking through the alley by her grandmother's house
> to go to the neighborhood store.
> She remembers the alley was dark and frightening,
> but that was the only way to get to the store.
> She had to be brave—her grandmother needed her.
> She remembers sitting and swinging on the porch swing.
> She remembers playing baseball in the field next to her grandmother's house.
> She remembers hot summers.
> She remembers....

To illustrate her poem, Tenesha brought copies of photographs of her grandmother's house and her grandmother, a close-up of the porch swing, a picture of herself holding a bat and wearing a cap.

Another student, Juan, wrote,

> He remembers tickling his mother to try and make her laugh.
> She didn't like it but it still didn't stop him from trying.

He remembers the drive to Mexico every summer
and how he couldn't wait to hug his grandmother.
He remembers the first time he tried to ride a bike and fell into a ditch.
He remembers his first fight and how scared he was, but he had to win.
He remembers walking to school for the very first time
and how he didn't want to let his mother's hand go when he got there.
He remembers....

To illustrate his poem, Juan brought copies of photographs of his grandmother, an old car, himself on his bicycle, and a recent photograph that was taken of him in front of his elementary school.

REFLECTION POINT

How could you alter this experience for different purposes? For example, could students create "remember" photo collage poems for characters from novels they are reading or for individuals they are reading about in their social studies texts and related texts?

ACTIVITY **8**

Creating Complete Memoirs Based Upon a Single Photograph

Now your students are ready to create complete memoirs based on a single photograph. Writing a memoir based upon a personal photograph gives students an opportunity to write about topics they know well: the events and people who make up the intense and memorable events of their lives. Writing with an image that focuses thought and provides a touchstone they can return to as the piece becomes more complex is also meaningful and helpful. The memoirs they write will be more than simple chronicles of the event or events.

Have your students select a photograph that tells something about a vivid or intense moment in their lives. Your students may choose one of the photographs they used in the photo collage they created to illustrate their "remember" photo collage poem, or they may bring in another photograph they want to write about. As students begin to work with their photographs, they will need to "read" what is in and what is behind the photograph. Viewing the photograph and reflecting on the content and meaning of what is contained and what is left out of the photograph helps writers to concentrate their writing on the single or related intense moments that make up a memoir.

When the students have their photograph in hand, provide them with quiet time to search the details within the image and jot down words, phrases, and notes to remind them of their observations and recollections. Have them examine the photograph carefully, listing details of what is seen and also what they remember and what they feel as they look at the photographs. Some students will want to talk to one another about their photographs. Talking is often the first step in formulating a piece you want to write. Then, with the talk in mind, and the photograph and notes in hand, students should begin to write, creating a richly detailed story about the event or events depicted in the photographs.

As writers focus on the image in the prewriting stage and then return to the image as they write their memoirs, they expand upon their descriptions, intuitions, and reflections related to the moments they write about. During the process, the writer may elaborate upon feelings and emotions, the writer may include events that are not in the photograph, the writer may enlighten readers further about the people in the photograph, but always it is the image that serves as the central core or the inspiration for the piece.

You and your students may want to decide on a length for the complete memoir. This could vary by grade level. You could also decide that the length will be determined by the student and the story he or she has to tell. You can then, through your questions and comments on the first draft, help students refine and expand upon the piece. In general, students who are writing about something they are interested in and something that they have chosen to write about will write more and be more willing to revise what they have written.

The following is an excerpt from a piece one of my students, Katlyn, wrote about a photograph of a pond (see Figure 3):

> Each year, sometimes twice a year, I return to the pond. I haven't been for over a year, but I can almost envision the walk there. Each year the streets get smaller and smaller and the neighbors wonder why I am not in school. Oranges and grapefruits hang from the trees and the sun beats down on my neck. In my hand I have a bag of crumbled bread that I will feed to the ducks. I see the same curved road. It is almost like a dream. The pond is just ahead.
>
> One of the first things I do when I get to my grandfather's house is walk to the pond to feed the ducks. I walk in the shade of the grand old trees that curve over the road. The ground is muddy and the ducks are loud as they swim in one large group. I throw bread toward them.

Another student, Joanie, wrote the following about a photograph of a house (see Figure 4)—or what she refers to as "unhouse":

> It was the first unhouse I had ever lived in. I remember going to school that morning and not realizing what walking out that door meant. I remember going home with my friend after school to trick-or-treat and my father picking me up afterwards to go to my new house. Not ours. He was not going to live there. We moved off the base on Halloween because my parents were getting divorced.

Figure 3
Photo of a Pond Used for Memoir Writing

Figure 4
Photo of a House Used for Memoir Writing

We had to sell many of our things and leave them behind because our unhouse was smaller and touched other unhouses. We sold the lawn mower because the unhouse had no yard; only a concrete slab path. My sister moved to a dorm on the college campus because the unhouse was too far away for her to ride her ten-speed to school.

My mother, my brother, and I moved to our new unhouse on Halloween. I was in second grade. My dad was gone, my sister was gone, and the lawn mower belonged to someone else. The unhouse had no garage and we could not walk to school anymore. We had to park the car under a canopy and Mom drove us to school. Mom had to work. The unhouse was not ours. The base house had not been ours either, but it was my family's home. I did not like our unhouse, but it became our home.

REFLECTION POINT

Before you ask your students to write complete memoirs, you may want to make decisions about the final product. Will you specify a number of paragraphs or pages? How do you want students to format the piece? Will you provide a rubric for students? How many class periods will they have to work on the piece? Do you want them to work independently outside of the classroom? As always, making expectations clear ahead of time can eliminate students' apprehension about meeting your expectations and allow them to focus on the process and product.

Conclusion

Allen and Labbo (2001) describe a similar experience to the memoir writing in this chapter as writing "cultural memoirs," a process in which they invite students to use "photographs of various influences on their lives" as the impetus for writing memoirs (p. 42). In general, our culture encompasses the ideas, customs, values, and practices that are passed down to us from generation to generation, though there may be other subforms of culture based upon social group, profession, and so on. For our purposes, when thinking about culture in relation to writing memoirs, we will view culture as being related to family influence. As students view, talk, and write, they become more cognizant of their own various cultures. Throughout these experiences students are learning how to "read" the photographs from their own lives to help them remember meaningful moments with clarity and detail. We begin by asking them to sort photographs in general, piecing together like events, settings, or "characters." Then, because we want to write memoirs, we help students develop concepts about what a memoir looks and sounds like by reading the memoirs of others, both picture books and excerpts from full-length texts. Our experiences in reading memoirs help us develop lists of the things we want to include in our own memoirs; we want to write about moments that we want to hold close and moments that we want to share with others. We want to use rich language so others can see the moment just as we remember it. Finally, we choose a photograph that holds the moment we want to write about. Reading the photographs and remembering and talking about these moments enables us to write memoirs that propel us backward in time and move us deeply.

Mark Faust (2004), who began taping and transcribing his grandmother's stories on her 90th birthday, writes about the implications of memoir telling and writing for educators, stating, "Activities that require students to pay attention to and craft their own memories can be directed toward helping them become more thoughtful readers and writers in other contexts" (p. 571). He also notes that as family members listened to the stories of GG, his grandmother, they were more likely to relate and critically evaluate events from their own past. Faust comments that "attending to the stories about our past causes us to reconstruct that past, an endeavor that has the potential to open up new avenues to the future" (p. 566). Preservice teachers studying with Allen and Labbo were asked to invite children in their practicum classrooms to participate in creating what might be termed a collaborative memoir. Children were asked to take pictures of things at home that were important to them. Families then worked together to write text to go along with the pictures in what Allen and Labbo (2001) termed a "school-home journal" (p. 44). Writing and sharing our memoirs helps us first to reach within ourselves and then to reach outside ourselves to others. When we look closely at photographs in order to use them as a basis for memoirs, we do as Perkins (1994) suggests when he describes the visual analysis of images. We "seek out not just what awaits but what *hides*, peering backstage at the pulleys, trap doors, and rain machines that help to create the on-stage illusion" (p. 22).

REFERENCES

Allen, J., & Labbo, L. (2001). Giving it a second thought: Making culturally engaged teaching culturally engaging. *Language Arts, 79*, 40–52.

Brandt, D. (2001). *Literacy in American lives.* New York: Cambridge University Press.

Faust, M. (2004). Mixing memory and desire: A family literacy event. *Journal of Adolescent & Adult Literacy, 47*, 564–572.

Kirby, D.L., & Kirby, D. (2007). *Memoir: A studio workshop approach.* Portsmouth, NH: Heinemann.

Kurstedt, R., & Koutras, M. (2000). *Teaching writing with picture books as models: Lessons and strategies for using the power of picture books to teach the elements of great writing in the upper grades.* New York: Scholastic.

New London Group. (2000). A pedagogy of multiliteracies: Designing social futures. In B. Cope & M. Kalantzis (Eds.), *Multiliteracies: Literacy learning and the design of social futures* (pp. 9–37). New York: Routledge.

Perkins, D.N. (1994). *The intelligent eye: Learning to think by looking at art.* Los Angeles: Getty Publications.

Welty, E. (1984). *One writer's beginnings.* Cambridge, MA: Harvard University Press.

Zinsser, W. (Ed.). (1987). *Inventing the truth: The art and craft of memoir.* Boston: Houghton Mifflin.

LITERATURE CITED

Auster, P. (1988). *The invention of solitude.* New York: Penguin.

Burandt, H., & Dale, S. (1997). *Tales from the homeplace: Adventures of a Texas farm girl.* New York: Henry Holt.

Cisneros, S. (2002). *Caramelo.* New York: Knopf.

Creech, S. (2000). *Fishing in the air.* New York: Joanna Cotler Books.

Giff, P.R. (2002). *Pictures of Hollis Woods.* New York: Random House.

Hart, E.T. (1999). *Barefoot heart: Stories of a migrant child.* Tempe, AZ: Bilingual Press.

Houston, G. (1992). *My great-aunt Arizona.* New York: HarperCollins.

Ingold, J. (1998). *Pictures, 1918.* New York: Harcourt Brace.

MacLachlan, P. (1991). *Three names.* New York: HarperCollins.

Mora, P. (1997). *Tomás and the library lady.* New York: Knopf.

Ringgold, F. (1993). *Dinner at Aunt Connie's house.* New York: Hyperion Books for Children.

Taulbert, C.L. (1989). *Once upon a time when we were colored.* New York: Penguin.

Watts, J.H. (1997). *Keepers.* New York: Lee & Low.

Wolff, T. (1989). *This boy's life: A memoir.* New York: Grove Press.

Yardley, J. (1991). *The red ball.* New York: Harcourt Brace Jovanovich.

CHAPTER 2

Understanding the Who and the Why: Reading Photographs to Write About Ourselves

HERE I AM LYING DOWN on a concrete bench in the sculpture garden of the Museum of Fine Arts. It's so peaceful here. I can feel the sun on my face and hear the rustle of the leaves in the bamboo screening fence that surrounds the garden. Jerry is off taking photographs for a project he's working on and I'm

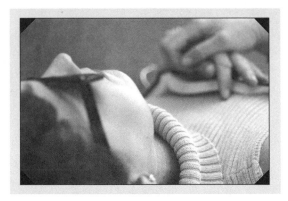

reading Jane Eyre for the fifth time. Right now, the book is facedown on my chest. I have my hands folded over it to protect the book and hold it close. I am thinking about how my readings of it change as I grow older.

I read Jane Eyre for the first time when I was in the fourth grade. I'm certain that there were many words I did not know the meaning of. I'm certain that there were many actions and innuendos that I did not know the meaning of. However, the heart of the story inspired me. To me, Jane Eyre was first and foremost a teacher. I dreamed that I would be a teacher. Later, when I was in junior high school and high school and reading the book for the second and third time, I thought that Jane's relationship with Edward Rochester was the most romantic thing I had ever known. I dreamed that I would become a governess and that a man just like him—mysterious, powerful, inexplicable, and somewhat gruff to everyone but me—would fall in love with me. Still later, when I was a file clerk/secretary for a local engineering company, I read the book for the fourth time. I noticed that at many times Jane's actions and choices were controlled by others. It seemed that everything she did was for the good of those around her. I dreamed that I could please those around me and still have control of my destiny. Now, in my fifth reading of Jane Eyre, I am drawn to her inner strength and to her understanding of herself and others. I contemplate her need to be loved and her need to be free to do what she must do. I admire her insistence that she live her life in a way that she herself can approve. Like Jane, I feel a need to be understood by others. Like Jane, I set standards for myself that I must uphold or I will not be satisfied. I dream of continuing the life I have now where love and freedom are intertwined.

When I think about a photograph that defines me, this one comes to mind immediately. All my life I have been a reader. As a young girl I was extremely shy and books were my sanctuary and my friends. Even now, as an older and more outgoing person, I am happiest when surrounded by my books. I treasure the stories in my books, the voices of people I will never know, the inspiration, the pain, the joy, the wonder. I treasure the books themselves, the way they feel and smell, their texture in my hands, and the way stacks of them form tables and walls. I revel in places I can read—stretched out on hammocks and concrete benches, curled up in wing chairs before the fireplace, lying down in the grass, lounging in a wicker chair on the porch, snuggled on an old couch with my dog, Franny, breathing softly in my ear. Books define me in many ways: what I read, how and when I read, the way I read, and why I read. I cannot imagine a life without books.

The photograph Jerry has taken of me thinking about reading is important to me. The feelings that I have when I look at the photograph and the way that I write about my associations with the photograph reveal a great deal about my own identity.

This chapter is devoted to learning experiences that will help your students question the unquestioned and, in doing so, discover and explore their identities as well as the words and images that define them. Taylor (2002) writes that "when used in research to understand how people define their selves and their world, photography often sheds light on the taken for granted or the unquestioned" (p. 123). Similarly, the photograph-based writing activities in this chapter will elicit thinking that goes beyond what is clearly there to go beyond basic understandings that may be taken for granted and to instead move to the "unquestioned." These experiences will require students to ask, What does this mean? and What does it say about me? As is exemplified in the vignette that opens this chapter, reflecting on the elements in a photograph—even elements in a photograph depicting an event that seems like a relatively insignificant moment in a person's life—can lead us to a greater understanding of ourselves.

Some of our students may choose to write about or create photographs that emphasize their cultural being or how they think their family and friends perceive their identity. For example, Allen and Labbo (2001) write about a student named Kelly who wanted to define "culture." Along with her writing she included a number of things: pictures, childhood stories, and poetry. Kelly stated that the artifacts "express who I am," saying, "I believe that the things that are most important to you make up your cultural being. Through family, friends, and life lessons, you are defined. To me, culture is a sense of who you are" (p. 45). When students are asked to create, collect, and analyze photographs that they feel represent aspects of themselves, they begin to focus on elements of their lives and cultures that make statements about or reveal more about their identities.

Working with photographs as a way to explore identity has been found to be particularly effective for teaching English-language learners (ELLs). Urdanivia-English (2001), herself a nonnative speaker of English, writes of the powerful experience of having her fifth-grade ELLs use photographs to write their personal histories. Taking photographs and developing understandings about themselves motivated and enabled Urdanivia-English and her students to make connections with family and with social studies. Similarly, Stanley (Isherwood & Stanley, 1994) refers to a project in which he worked to integrate photography and the national curriculum in Great Britain. He notes that engagement was a powerful aspect for students:

> the involvement of the self in the processes of reading and making photographs, the identification of the self in the process of producing photographs and consuming them. It is about what happens when and where the self and the photograph meet. Identification of the self in the process of looking involves understanding how the self is made to look and how the self is represented. (p. 33)

In many ways, the activities in this chapter build upon the experiences in chapter 1. When we write memoirs, we focus upon a unique moment or moments in our lives; we reflect on the meaning of events and our relationships with others. When we write to define ourselves and our identities, we take this examination to the next level by looking inward. We alter the central focus of writing memoir, where our thoughts are based in what we were and what has been, to a focus on identity: what we *are* and what we *may become*. We reflect and write to understand and clarify ourselves. These two types of writing work well together. For many writers it is beneficial to work from the outside to the inside—from the general or whole life to the specific, individual, or inner life. For that reason we have begun with memoir writing before moving to address writing that helps us define ourselves.

In this chapter we will examine and reflect upon ways that we can use photographs to help our students develop concepts about identity and write about themselves as they do the following:

- Explore issues of identity by examining novels and short stories in which the main characters examine their identities
- Examine texts that link photography and identity
- Write poems about their names

- Create a photo collage representing scenes from literature
- Create a Photo-Life Map
- Create an essay exploring identity using the analytical tools developed in the previous learning experiences

Exploring Identity Through Literature

What makes us who we are? Is it the people we know and love? The community in which we live? The things that happen in our life? In order to begin thinking about people and how they come to be, you and your students can engage in a shared reading or a Readers Theatre performance reading of excerpts from a novel that explores issues of identity, such as Sandra Cisneros's (1984) *The House on Mango Street*, Paul Fleischman's (1997) *Seedfolks*, or other books that take readers inside the lives of people in a community or neighborhood. See Table 4 for a list of novels students might want to read to find out about other young people exploring themselves and their identities.

Shared reading occurs when the teacher reads aloud to the students while the students follow along in their own copies of the text. During this process

Table 4
Suggested Novels for Using Literature to Explore Identity

Alvarez, J. (2002). *How Tía Lola came to (visit) stay*. New York: Knopf.
Alvarez, J. (2006). *Finding miracles*. New York: Knopf.
Banerjee, A. (2006). *Looking for Bapu*. New York: Wendy Lamb Books.
Banerjee, A. (2006). *Maya running*. New York: Wendy Lamb Books.
Canales, V. (2007). *The tequila worm*. New York: Wendy Lamb Books.
Cofer, J.O. (1996). *An island like you: Stories from the barrio*. New York: Orchard Books.
Hamilton, V. (1992). *Cousins*. New York: Scholastic.
Hamilton, V. (2006). *M.C. Higgins, the great*. New York: Simon & Schuster.
Johnson, A. (2000). *Heaven*. New York: Simon & Schuster.
Namioka, L. (2006). *Mismatch*. New York: Delacorte.
Namioka, L. (2007). *April and the dragon lady*. San Diego, CA: Harcourt.
Ryan, P.M. (2005). *Becoming Naomi León*. New York: Scholastic.
Smith, G.L. (2005). *Ninjas, piranhas, and Galileo*. Boston: Little, Brown.
Soto, G. (2006). *Accidental love*. San Diego: Harcourt.
Weeks, S. (2004). *So b. it*. New York: HarperCollins.
Yep, L. (2001). *Angelfish*. New York: Penguin.

you may have student volunteers "jump in" and take over the reading for a page or two. Readers Theatre is an experience in which participants have more than one opportunity to read the text as they prepare to perform it. Readers may highlight character dialogue in a narrative and choose someone else to read the subtext between the dialogue. Some props may be used, but Readers Theatre can be quite effective with students sitting together on stools or chairs. Students might sit or stand with their backs to the audience, turning to face the audience as they say their lines. As students become more practiced with Readers Theatre, they may create their own written pieces based upon novels, short stories, or informational texts describing a certain period of time or course of events. I often read several excerpts from Sandra Cisneros's *The House on Mango Street* with my students. I choose this book because it contains short, beautifully detailed written illustrations of a wide variety of fascinating characters.

Once you select a novel, choose pages or chapters to form a cohesive excerpt from the novel. If possible, include introductory and concluding thoughts from the novel and a representation of several characters. Then, engage your students in a shared reading or a Readers Theatre performance of the excerpt. For example, when using *The House on Mango Street*, I engaged students in a shared reading of the chapters titled "My Name," "Meme Ortiz," "Those Who Don't," "Elenita, Cards, Palm, Water," "Edna's Ruthie," and "Mango Says Goodbye Sometimes." The first and last excerpts framed the reading experience, serving as a beginning and conclusion.

While students are listening or participating in the reading as a class, have students work to create a group list of any questions they have, the things they may notice about characters or events, or the personal connections they are making to the text on a large sheet of bulletin board paper or an easel board. It is helpful to have your students do this where all can see what is written so that the students will develop their understanding of the text collaboratively. For example, as my students read excerpts from *The House on Mango Street*, they recorded their observations or questions on a large sheet of bulletin board paper posted at the front of the room, and we sat in a circle around the paper. The students could get up and write at any time during the reading. To avoid confusion and noise, I asked that only one person get up at a time. As we read the chapter "My Name," Carmen wrote, "I love the idea of writing about our names and how we feel about them." Maria added, "I guess a name is more than just a name...it's who you are." Later, when we read "Elenita, Cards, Palm, Water," several students made personal connections. Ramona wrote, "Palm Sunday crosses, holy candles, my great grandmother's house." Cecelia provided further insight with the words "I remember my grandma rubbing an egg and some herbs over our bodies when we were sick (evil eye, we thought)." Finally, Loretta concluded, "Generally most Latinos (first generation or better yet, recent arrival) are superstitious."

When you and your students generate ideas during reading, it is likely that you will have several sheets of their thoughts on which you can base discussion. It may take more than one experience for students to feel comfortable with writing their thoughts and ideas where everyone can see them. Some students may be more comfortable in the familiar territory of teacher-led discussion. Be patient and provide more than one opportunity for them to engage. You will find that discussions based upon student ideas become events in which more students participate at a higher level of thinking (Van Horn, 2001). Students who participate in a discussion based on excerpts such as these from *The House on Mango Street* may talk about their own superstitions and family customs. The chapter titled "My Name," for instance, may inspire them to write about their own names.

You can delve deeper into issues related to defining ourselves and understanding our identities through the reading of short stories on this topic. There are a number of stories to choose from in collections such as *Baseball in April and Other Stories* (Soto, 1990), *Connections: Short Stories by Outstanding Writers for Young Adults* (Gallo, 1989), *Sixteen Short Stories by Outstanding Writers for Young Adults* (Gallo, 1984), *Who Do You Think You Are? Stories of Friends and Enemies* (Rochman & McCampbell, 1993), *Gorilla, My Love* (Bambara, 1992), and *Once Upon a Childhood: Stories and Memoirs of American Youth* (Solomon & Panetta, 2004). Further information about each book can be found in the Appendix.

After you choose a short story about identity appropriate for your students, provide background knowledge about the author, if appropriate, and remind students that they are accumulating ideas and experiences to build their concept of identity and self-defining issues. For example, in one of my classes, we read a piece titled "Black, White, and Jewish" taken from a book called *Black, White, and Jewish: Autobiography of the Shifting Self* (Walker, 2001).

We began with my reading information about the author, Rebecca Walker. Walker, named by *Time* magazine as one of the 50 future leaders in America, is the daughter of Pulitzer Prize—winning black author Alice Walker and Mel Leventhal, a white civil rights lawyer. The excerpt we read from *Black, White, and Jewish* chronicles the first months after her parents divorce, her move with her mother to a tiny apartment, her start in a new school, and her struggles to decide whether she should emphasize her black or her white heritage. She relays her feelings through incidents that on the surface may be read as humorous but that, in fact, may be painful indeed. As might be expected, there will be much to talk about following the reading.

During the reading of the short story, invite students to reflect. When you are interested in focusing on identity and self-defining issues, it is helpful as students read to have them channel their thinking in a two-column dialogue journal entry in their writer's journals. Column headings for the two-column entry should be "What I Read" (direct excerpts or notes taken from the text) and "What I Think" (personal connections to what I have read and new understandings). With these headings you are giving students the opportunity to notice what stands out for them in the text and to think further as they copy or paraphrase the text. Readers can then read these words or sentences in the left column of the journal entry and write about connections or understandings that are prompted by the words. Figure 5 illustrates sample two-column dialogue entries from the journals of several of my students.

Hold a discussion in which students may share their excerpts, notes, and reflections with others as a whole class, in small groups, or with partners. However, be aware that students may or may not want to talk about what they have written in their writer's journals. In this particular instance my students seemed reluctant to share out loud in class. Instead they chose to hand in their journals and allowed me to respond to them one-on-one. Your students may not be ready to divulge this level of personal information in a whole-class discussion.

Figure 5
Sample Two-Column Dialogue Journal Entries

What I Read (Direct excerpts or notes taken from the text)	What I Think (Personal connections to what I have read; new understandings)
I'm just alone with all of these other kids with names and faces but not much else.	High school life has been tough. Not really connecting with anyone. We're like strangers in the night.
I don't know what I am and I don't know how to be not what he thinks I am. I don't know how to be a not black girl.	I think she is losing herself and trying to find herself through the eyes of others.
(same as above)	I remember when I started school after I moved. I was put in regular classes. Everyone was different. No one talked Spanish, there was no hint of the Mexican culture, so I tried everything to not be Mexican. I pretty much turned my back on who I was.
This year I'm paranoid. I don't trust any of my friends all the way.	That's how I felt after my dad left. My sense of trust diminished.
(same as above)	She feels she can't trust anyone and I'm in the same situation. I had a friend that broke my trust so I can relate to her (Rebecca).

ACTIVITY 2

Examining Texts That Link Photographs and Identity

In order to help your students make connections between visual and written images of self and identity, it is important to examine texts that link photographs and identity. Specifically, these are texts that typically feature a central character who is struggling with his or her identity formation and in which there is a direct connection made between the character's actions, this struggle, and photographs. In addition, another feature of these texts is photographs of people that are used to illustrate short statements, narratives, or poetry that explores the nature of being and identity formation. Therefore, collect texts that feature links between photographs and identity, and plan to share these texts with your students. You might choose to begin your analysis and collection of ideas about photographs with the reading of a picture book, such as *The Sea Chest* by Toni Buzzeo (2002) or *When Lightning Comes in a Jar* by Patricia Polacco (2002; further information about each book can be found in the Appendix).

As you move away from the picture books you may choose to read aloud to students as a class or have students work in small groups with each text, rotating the text from group to group while students note their observations in their writer's journals. For example, you might begin with a whole-class reading of the novel *Journey* by Patricia MacLachlan (1991), or you might prefer to book talk the novel by reading several excerpts and have students choose to read it on their own. To help readers begin to think about the "truth" in photographic images, start with the section in the beginning in which the boy, Journey, is looking at family photographs with his grandmother. Journey examines a photograph of a family picnic. He notices that his mother, who has left him with his grandparents, seems detached from the family even at that time. She is not looking at or interacting with others. She looks unhappy or discontented. Journey's grandmother remarks that "the camera knows" (p. 11).

Following that, you may want to read the pages of the novel in which Journey is visiting his friend Cooper's house and looking at photographs. He tells Cooper's mother that his grandfather has told him that "pictures show us the truth sometimes" (p. 56). Mrs. McDougal shows Journey a photograph of her family in which they look like the "perfect family" (p. 56), even though one of her brothers is pinching "the devil" (p. 56) out of her.

To build upon the ideas you are formulating, continue by reading the beginning pages of Patricia Reilly Giff's (2002) novel *Pictures of Hollis Woods*. In these pages Hollis remembers when she was 6 years old and her teacher, Mrs. Evans, asked the students to cut out pictures that began with the letter *W*. Hollis, who was a foster child, cut out a picture of a family. Mrs. Evans spoke sharply to Hollis and drew an *X* over her picture, telling her there was nothing in the picture that started with a *W*. Hollis started to respond, "What about W for wish, or W for want, or W for 'Wouldn't it be loverly,' like the song the music teacher had taught us?" (p. 1).

Talk about projects in which photographers and authors have taken pictures of people and made these pictures the base for writing about identity and self. For example, with older students you might share *Things I Have to Tell You: Poems and Writing by Teenage Girls*, edited by Betsy Franco (2001), in which black-and-white photographs of adolescent girls accompany writing by teenage girls. Photographs by Nina Nickles of girls jumping rope, talking in the bathroom, putting on makeup, skipping rocks, and leaving home to go to a school dance accompany poems titled "I'm Sayin'," "Be Perfect," "Contemplating Fat and Thin..." and "Just Another Girl."

Students of all ages might enjoy looking at *Revealing Character: Texas Tintypes* by Robb Kendrick (2005). A tintype is a photographic technique that originated in the 1800s, in which one must stand perfectly still for seven seconds without blinking while being photographed. Every other page in the book contains a sepia-toned tintype of a modern-day cowboy or cowgirl. On the page opposite the tintype, readers learn something about the individual. Direct quotes are included with most tintypes. For example, the book includes a photograph of Zach Davis, who works at the King Ranch in Texas, USA; Zach rests on one knee in front of a circular bale of hay taller than himself. He is dressed in a felt cowboy hat, checker-patterned shirt, denim jacket, jeans, and leather chaps that come to his knees. He looks solemnly into the camera. In the accompanying text, Zach tells us,

> You can't close a man in with four walls. You need the open space to appreciate the nature of our country. This is true freedom and the American way of life. Take a man's freedom, and you take his heart. (p. 142)

Further information about each of the previously described books can be found in the Appendix. After examining and talking about the texts you have selected, hold a discussion in which your students can share their thoughts and ideas about photographs. Pull their ideas together for a class listing of thoughts that can remain posted in the room as you engage in related learning experiences.

In my class, we agreed that "sometimes the picture knows the truth," and other times "the truth is behind the picture, not within it." Consuela noted that "you can talk to people through your photographs." We started to list things we will want to think about as we write about photographs: What is there? What is not there? How does this represent or symbolize me? As we began to think about photographs that would define us, Juan noted, "We can also have photographs of things that we want." We agreed that we can be defined or our identities may be reflected in things that we strive to attain. At this point we began to pull our thoughts and ideas together—an important first step in creating a piece that will combine visual and written texts.

REFLECTION POINT

Can you think of other texts that include meaningful references to photographs or that integrate photographs and language? How else might you get students to think about and talk about the meaning of photographs?

My Self, My Name: Students Writing Poems About Their Names

"My Name" is a chapter from *The House on Mango Street* in which Cisneros (1984) writes about a young girl named Esperanza. Esperanza tells us what her name means in English and Spanish. She describes her name by the way it looks, "a muddy color" (p. 10), and by what it sounds like, "the Mexican records my father plays on Sunday mornings when he is shaving, songs like sobbing" (p. 10). She relates the history of her name and how she came to be called Esperanza, beginning with the words "It was my great-grandmother's name" (p. 10). She describes the way her name sounds when others say it aloud. She tells us what her name is made of, "silver" (p. 11). She tells us that unlike her sister Magdalena who can become Nenny at home, she is always Esperanza. She has no nickname or other name. She concludes by telling us what she would be called if she could choose her own name, the name that would express "the real me" (p. 11). After conducting a close reading of the text, invite your students to tell you what they noticed about the steps that the author takes the character through to tell you about her name. You may want to keep a record of what they say on a class list where all can see it. This class list can be used as a reference point.

Next, working with student input, organize or highlight the responses that make up the format or outline of the poem they will write. Then, have students begin to draft a poem about their name using this format or outline. Before you have students begin writing, instruct them to title their pieces with their names followed by the street on which they live. For example, a piece might be titled "Tabitha Henry, The House on Seahorse Lane."

In order to provide an opportunity to view and think about visual texts, you may want to invite the students to include a photograph of themselves with the piece. When students have had an opportunity to do some initial thinking about their poems and have written down some ideas, suggest that they think of a way they can be photographed that tells something about their identity. These photographs can be taken in the classroom with a digital camera, or you might use single-use cameras. Students may bring in objects that define them or pose in ways that suggest what is important to them. For example, someone might be photographed holding their favorite book. A student who is in the drama club might pose in costume. As an alternative students might bring in a photograph of themselves from home. They might be asked to study the photograph to help them think about their name and what it does or does not reveal about them.

The following is a poem created by one of my students, Melissa:

In English my name means "giver of love."
In Spanish it means dropping the "M" and pronouncing it "elissa."
It means, "help me," "come," "finish," and "STOP!"
It is like a cloudy day with scattered tear drops all around.
It is the duties of the only daughter and middle child.
It is the calling of the woman who struggles to love, protect,
shelter, and guide a two year old.

Another student, Jennifer Angelica, wrote the following poem about the way her changed feelings about her name represent her acknowledgment and joy in who she is (see Figure 6 for the photo that accompanied her poem):

I am Hispanic, born in El Salvador.
My first name is so American. I wish I had a first name that was more Hispanic,
more like my middle name, Angelica.
I have come to a point in my life when I am proud to be Hispanic.
When I was younger I would hate for people to know my middle name was Angelica. Now
I think Angelica is beautiful and Jennifer is plain.
But I am Jennifer.
No longer the Jennifer not wanting to be Hispanic,
but the Jennifer everyone looks at and says "She is so Hispanic."

Figure 6
Jennifer Angelica's Photo to Accompany Name Poem

I know it.
I am proud of it.
I have learned to be proud of who I am, an American and a Hispanic,
and it shows through in my two names,
Jennifer Angelica.

Younger students might want to mount their pieces on house-shaped cutouts and post them in the hallways of the school as if they were homes on a street in a neighborhood. Older students might want to compile their pieces in a class book, or submit them to the school literary journal or yearbook.

REFLECTION POINT

Suppose you choose to read excerpts from Fleischman's (1997) *Seedfolks* or another text that will not, of course, include the chapter "My Name." Could your students respond using photographs and writing in another way as they think about identity and how they define themselves? For example,

Seedfolks is about people who live in an apartment house in the city and how each of them contributes to a community garden. Could your students bring in a photograph of something in their home or community that represents their identity or helps to define them and write about that?

ACTIVITY 4

Creating a Photo Collage Representing Scenes From Literature

In this activity, students will create collages that represent scenes, chapters, and/or major events in literature; by doing this, they are engaged with making decisions about which elements to include and how to symbolize these elements with an image. This is an important scaffolding activity that will help students begin using the thinking and decision-making processes they will use when they create Photo-Life Maps that represent themselves (see Activity 5) and later when they choose and write about a single photograph that defines them (see Activity 6). You might work with students to divide a short story into "scenes," and then have small groups work together to create a photo collage representing a particular scene. This activity may also be done with a full-length text, in which case students would choose chapters or major events to depict in their collages. The collages could consist of images clipped from magazines or from electronic sources, or they could be original photographs taken by the students.

Have students read a short story or a chapter or event from a full-length text about identity and then talk about the function of scenes in a play. (Depending upon your students and the choices you have made in the previous activities, you may have students read a piece they have not read before, or you can opt to use one you have read together as a class.) Then, skim the text once again with students and talk about where a "scene" might begin and end. As you discuss these ideas, ask students to express the reasons for their choices and be sure to draw attention to examples in which students suggest changing scenes due to natural transitions, such as a change in setting or a flashback. Also note when students suggest changing scenes or isolating scenes to heighten the importance of a particular event.

Next, using the scenes established by the class, break the class into pairs and assign or allow partners to choose the scene they will work with. Partners will reread the scene together, making note of important characters, settings, events, and details that they may include in their photo collages. Then, partners may clip photographs from magazines, locate electronic copies of photographs, or take their own photographs to create their photo collages, placing images in a cohesive, meaningful manner to represent their scene from the text. Finally, when the photo collage is complete, instruct partners to write a list of the images depicted in the collage and the meaning behind them. Have the whole class gather at a central location and view the photo collages placed in the sequence in which they actually occur in the story. Then have the partners read aloud their scenes to the group, explaining their photo collage meanings.

To model this process, I will share an experience from one of my own classes in which we used the text *Black, White, and Jewish: Autobiography of the Shifting Self* (Walker, 2001) as the basis for photo collages. First, we divided the text into 14 scenes. Most scenes consisted of one to two long paragraphs. Talking about scenes enabled us to focus on how the author signaled transitions. We also talked about how some events felt important enough to be contained in a separate scene, even though the setting or time might be the same as in the previous paragraph. For example, Rebecca takes us into her new school and down the hallway into her first class with Mrs. Leone. A transition occurs when she walks down the hallway with her classmates to Mr. Ward's music class. Here, as she begins to talk about music class, we formed a new scene. Even though she is still in music class when she begins to talk about Bryan Katon, a boy she likes, we moved to another scene. The description and study of Bryan merit their own scene. The smaller scenes enabled students to focus on locating and representing important details without being overwhelmed by too many events, objects, and/or characters.

When the photo collages were complete, I asked each group to write about what they included in their collages and why they had included the photos they used. I asked them to describe how each element of the photo collage symbolizes something from the book or relates to an event in the book. Later, we gathered at a large table in the center of the room. I asked the students to place their collages around the table in the order in which the scenes occur in the book. I read each scene aloud, and following the reading of each scene, we clustered together and looked at the photo collage representing the scene while the "artists" described their decision-making process.

Then, I read aloud the final scene in which Rebecca, who has asked her mother not to come to see her in the school play, realizes the impact of what she has done. Shame and sadness wash over her as she thinks, "Even though everyone says I was good, my mama, the one with the most important voice, can never say this to me. Shame sticks to me like sweat" (Walker, in Solomon & Panetta, 2004, p. 299).

Figure 7
Chrysala and Deena's Photo Collage Based on Walker's *Black, White, and Jewish*

Figure 7 is a photo collage created by my students Chrysala and Deena depicting the final scene from *Black, White, and Jewish* that we chose to look at. Chrysala and Deena described the images and their meaning by explaining,

> The door shows that she is trapped by who she is. The letters L-O-V-E at a diagonal across the collage show when she realized how important it would have been to have her mom attend the play. There are three girls in the collage. The first sad girl is Rebecca. The two other girls are her classmates who are happy because they see their family there at the play. The fog represents the gloominess Rebecca feels. The orange colors are the heat inching beneath her face as she is sad and ashamed.

REFLECTION POINT

As you might imagine, the piece that you choose to have your students read and create a collage for should relay the story of someone who is reflecting on his or her own identity. Are there other short stories you know of that would be appropriate for your students?

Creating the Photo-Life Map

The Photo-Life Map activity is a way for students to brainstorm ideas with multiple photographs in much the same way that one might brainstorm a list of characteristics when writing a piece about the self. Participating in this activity will help students prepare for the photo-selection process that will be necessary when they narrow down their choices to one or two photographs for writing the final essay about a photograph that defines them. When the students have collected their photographs, they will be ready to begin constructing a Photo-Life Map. Merriam-Webster defines *map* as a "representation usually on a flat surface of the whole or part of an area" and as "something that represents with clarity...." When you ask students to create a Photo-Life Map, you ask them to use a series of photographs to represent themselves with clarity. Using poster board or large sheets of watercolor or drawing paper, students will mount their photographs with rubber cement or photo corners to create a "map" of their own lives and identities. Photographs may be placed in ways that indicate an order of importance. Underneath each photograph students will write a paragraph explaining how the picture defines or represents their individual identity.

If you want to help your students write essays about photographs that define them, you should spend some time talking with them about the meaning of *define*. For many students the word *define* or *definition* calls to mind instances in which they may have been asked to look up meanings for a list of words and to write beside the words the definitions from the dictionary.

In my experience, I find it helpful at times to stand at the overhead projector and ask my students to generate ideas on a topic while I write down all that they say. When we have generated all the ideas that we can, we can spend some time talking about what is written and what it might mean. For example, when I ask my students, "What does the word *define* mean to you?" they reply that it means to "represent," that it is the "components or pieces, the what and who that gives you meaning" and that to define yourself is to think about "what and who you are."

Because you will ask students to collect or generate photographs that define them, it is important that they collaborate with you to create a shared understanding of what you mean by this. Such a discussion helps us move forward with particular objectives in mind, for example, "I am looking for photographs that represent some of the aspects of my character, photographs that represent things about me that others may or may not know, and/or photographs that represent what is important to me—what I value and what I believe." With these ideas in mind, students can begin to think about using photographs that help define or represent the aspects, living or otherwise, that reveal what and who they are and why they are meaningful.

First, let your students know well in advance that they will need to bring in at least a dozen photographs that contain people, animals, elements, or structures that represent or define them. Students may search through family albums and copy or scan their photographs, or they may take new photographs specifically for this purpose. Because you are going to ask students to create a Photo-Life Map with these photographs, you'll want to ensure that no one is using irreplaceable photographs.

When the students have brought in their photographs to class, it may be helpful to ask them to choose one and talk about it to the whole class or to a partner. I like to demonstrate this for the students with a photograph of my own. For example, I might project the photograph of a stack of twigs and vines such as in Figure 8. As my students and I looked at the image, I would

Figure 8
Photo of Twigs and Vines Used to Demonstrate Ideas for Photo-Life Map

talk about how this photograph defines or represents an element of myself, saying,

> Last week while I was in Galveston I noticed this pile of twigs. I thought about it all morning while I ran errands. Before I left town I circled back and parked so I could take a picture of it. I ended up taking a half dozen or more photographs from different angles. Why the twigs? For as long as I can remember I have loved flowers and trees and plants. When I was a young girl I used to braid my hair with flowers. I can "lose" myself for hours in the garden, pulling rotted leaves and dead flowers off of plants, weeding, clipping bushes into imaginative shapes, sitting on a bench and just listening to the garden. I have a collection of twigs that I like to put in vases with or without flowers. Once, when I traveled to Colorado, I noticed some twigs that had a reddish color to them on the ground. I collected as many as I could find and packed them in my carry-on garment bag to take home with me. I eat with flatware shaped like twigs. Twigs represent my love of nature. They are young branches or pieces of trees so they might represent my desire to care for and protect people while they are learning and growing.

Similarly, I encourage you to use your own photograph and your own thoughts and reflections in a way that is geared to the students you teach.

Next, ask your students to turn to a partner or to the whole class and share their thoughts about one of the photographs they have with them, as it often helps to talk about their ideas before writing. After this experience invite students to jot down ideas in their journals about each of their photographs. As they write have them ask themselves, What does this represent? and How does this define me?

When students have had an opportunity to talk about one of their photographs, they can then write about this "talk." Students should write several sentences to a paragraph underneath or beside each photograph. What is written should explain how the picture defines or represents the students' individual identity. For example, one of my students, Marny, wrote about a sunset she saw while driving past a lake (see Figure 9). She included a title for this photograph, "A snapshot of God's painting splattered across the lake's sky," and wrote,

> This sunset reminds me of how I want to appreciate life's moments. God had to be thinking about how stressful life here on earth can be. He probably wanted to share something beautiful for us to see so we would relax for a few minutes. I see God popping and cracking his gigantic fingers, getting ready to splatter the sky with this sunset.

With these words Marny let us know how important it is for her to value everything she encounters and that she is a person who reflects on her faith.

Another student might write about the importance of having a home. For example, the following paragraph is a sample of what might be written about a photograph of a house:

Figure 9
Marny's Photo of a Sunset for Photo-Life Map

This is our first house. When we first moved here my family had to live in an apartment in a not very nice neighborhood. We had to live with my aunt and my three cousins. It was pretty crowded and there was no place to go to be by yourself. There was no privacy at all. Everyone worked to save up for our first house. I even donated some of the money I made doing chores for the neighbors. This house is important to all of us. To my parents it means that they finally achieved their dream of giving us a place we could call home here in the United States. For me it means that we are going to make it here. For me it is a place where I can be myself and be with just my family if I want to. I feel safe here in my new home; my first house in America.

As students study their photographs and write their thoughts about them, they begin to see that the images and the language they put with them characterize their identities and reveal how they see themselves. Students can narrow their focus to one or two of these photographs for the photograph essay.

REFLECTION POINT

As teachers, it is often helpful for us to engage in an activity ourselves before we experience it along with our students. Choose a photograph or photographs that you think represent an aspect of your own identity and write about the photograph(s) in a similar manner to that which you read about here. If possible, choose something that you can later share with your students as you demonstrate the process.

Writing an Essay About a Photograph That Defines Us

The final activity for this chapter is an essay based on a distinctive photograph that defines who a student is as an individual and represents how he or she sees himself or herself. You may ask your students to expand upon their ideas from the Photo-Life Map about multiple photographs, or you may have them choose a single photograph to write about. When working with younger students, it may be simpler to concentrate on a single photograph.

Writing about what defines us and how we conceive our identity is intensely personal. When I began to work with my students, I did not know that they would trust me enough to allow me to see them in this way. I read about friends who had grown apart because one had made choices the other could not sanction, about young people who were seeing their parents or their brothers or sisters in pain and who did not know how to help them, about young people who felt that no one understood or cared about them, and about young men and women who simply wanted to be accepted in the world for who and what they are—I was completely overwhelmed. This is something you will want to prepare for. I believe it is a sign of trust when our students reveal themselves in this way. It may also be an appeal for help or for understanding. If you read something that you feel is such an appeal, then you can follow up with the student in a face-to-face conversation. It is important for our students to know that we have read what they have written and that we care.

Reflecting on Previous Writing Experiences and Designing a Format for the Essay

Before beginning to write essays about a photograph or photographs, it is critical to reflect on the language that has been used throughout this unit to describe photographs in order to decide how to proceed. When writing poems about names based upon readings of excerpts from Sandra Cisneros's (1984) *The House on Mango Street*, the focus centered on words that projected images of what students' names look and sound like, and students thought about the history of their names. When responding in writer's journals to readings of novels or short stories dealing with identity issues, the emphasis was on personal connections or new understandings. When writing about the photo collages made to represent scenes from literature, students noted the symbolic or representational meaning of the images chosen for the collage. Finally, when writing about a collection of personal photographs for the Photo-Life Map, students created a paragraph explaining how the picture defined or represented their individual identity.

Reflecting on these experiences, it is possible to create a working outline or format of the essay with your students. Consider the following list as a guideline that can be added to or altered by individual writers as needed.

- Begin with a description of the visual elements of the photograph.
- Discuss the symbolic or representational meaning of the image.
- Describe what the image sounds or feels like.
- Reflect on personal connections/personal history related to the image.
- Discuss how the photograph defines or represents an aspect of your individual identity.
- If applicable, close with a note about new understandings.

Writing based upon this outline helps students use a photograph to come to an understanding and discuss their emerging identities. We can see how this happens if we reflect back on my chapter-opening vignette about the photograph of myself lying on the bench holding the book *Jane Eyre* close to my heart. As I described what was in the photograph, I began to think about what the elements meant to me. That led me to think about the book and the placement of the book over my heart, and what that might symbolize. As I began to think about my personal connections to the book and my "history" with the book, I began to chronicle the various meanings I have made from my numerous readings of the book. Finally, as I thought about the book and then books in general, I was able to come to some conclusions and new understandings about who I am as a person. When we break down the process in this way, carefully chosen photographs can help us think and write about ourselves.

Some of you may prefer to create your own guidelines for the essay ahead of time rather than constructing them along with your students. That is certainly an option and may help you to address your students' individual needs. Regardless of whether you choose to engage in the process described below or whether you create your own guidelines, it will be helpful for your students if you demonstrate or model the process of writing to the guidelines described in the following section.

Demonstrating the Process of Writing an Essay Based Upon a Single Photograph

Begin by either working with your students to create an example as a whole class or by demonstrating the process, writing where the students can see the process taking place. In this case, because your students are planning to write an essay about a photograph that defines them, the piece cannot be written as a group but rather individually. Therefore, demonstrate the process by writing a piece of your own while your students observe.

Project a photographic image and, using the list on page 64 as an outline, demonstrate the process of writing an essay about a photograph, pausing occasionally to verbalize the thinking that you are doing during the writing process. You can talk about what you are doing during or after the writing. For example, I projected the hopscotch board image in Figure 10 so my students could view it as I wrote. Later, students can use this guideline list as an organizer for their own piece. It will be helpful to your students if you create a similar organizer based upon this one or an alternate plan that you develop yourself to meet your students' needs. The piece I wrote as I demonstrated the process for my students can be found in Figure 11.

Naturally, as I wrote I would have to stop and think. While demonstrating this for my students, I tried to think to myself out loud. As I wrote each section or as I moved into the next section of the essay, I went back and reread

Figure 10
Photo of Hopscotch Board to Demonstrate Essay-Writing Process to Students

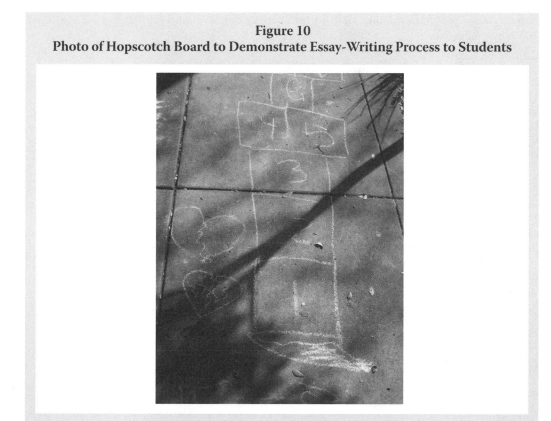

Figure 11
Written Demonstration of Essay-Writing Process

Begin with a description of the visual elements of the photograph.
Here is a chalk-drawn hopscotch board scribed on a rough old sidewalk on Church Street. Two hearts are drawn to the left of the hopscotch trail. One has a jagged line scrawled through the center and the other encloses twisting, line-drawn confetti. Delicate palm frond shadows reach out to trace the edge of the board.

Discuss the symbolic or representational meaning of the image.
One heart is sadness and the other is joy. The hopscotch board is childhood; a road we draw to take us to adulthood. A path filled with joyous adventure and anxious trepidation.

Describe what the image sounds or feels like.
I plant my feet at the end of the board, just before the square containing the number "1." Whispering, two, three, four, five, six, seven, eight, nine, ten. I look around to see that no one is watching, slip off my sandals, and then nudge them to the grass at the edge of the sidewalk. The concrete is bumpy under my feet.

  I reach into my pocket and pull out the smooth mother-of-pearl inside of an oyster shell I keep with me. Tossing the shell I hop on one foot and then on two, moving awkwardly from one square to the next until I reach the number five square, where the shell has landed. Bending to pick up the shell while balancing on one foot, wobbling but not falling. Rotating and hopping back to square four on two feet, sound softly patting the sidewalk, to three, to two, to one, and then off the board. Heart thumping in my ears; happy heart filled with confetti, not sad heart cut by a jagged line.

Reflect on personal connections/personal history related to the image.
When I was a little girl I played hopscotch on the driveway in front of our house on Kingfisher Street. I loved to play hopscotch because my mother had taught me how to play and, frequently, would play with me on hot summer afternoons when the cicadas whirred above us in the old ash tree in the middle of the yard. I always drew my hopscotch trail on the driveway rather than the sidewalk because I was a superstitious little girl. I heartily believed what Janet Alexander had told me, "Step on a crack, break your mother's back!"

Discuss how the photograph defines or represents an aspect of your individual identity.
This photograph of a hopscotch board with the hearts drawn beside it represents several aspects of my identity. The pathway of the board, the aspect of chance involved with where the oyster shell lands and whether I can remain balanced on one foot and hop to two at the right moments, is the part of me that would like not to be, but always is, somewhat anxious and fearful about what lies ahead on the trail. The positioning of the board on the sidewalk is the part of me that wants to believe that things will turn out if I am careful, work hard enough, and don't step on the cracks. The drawings beside the board are the part of me that lives for happy endings and hearts filled with confetti.

If applicable, close with a note about new understandings.
As I reflect on this photograph and what it may represent about me, I realize that I can move forward if I keep my worries contained to a certain area; perhaps inside a hopscotch board on the sidewalk in front of my house!

what I had written—I changed the word *box* to *square* for continuity. I added the word *to* before each number in the third section to try to establish a rhythmic patting sound with the numbers. Sometimes a student would suggest something to me and I would consider that and put it down if it worked. Even though it may have felt slightly uncomfortable to reflect, compose, and edit in front of a group of people, I did this to make overt the hidden aspects of writing. This is a process similar to the one in which I enact think-alouds and talk about the strategies I use when I am reading out loud.

REFLECTION POINT

You might want to try this for yourself. If you have not demonstrated the writing process in front of your students in the past, it might help to start with something short—a sentence or two—or to think about what you will write and make a few notes ahead of time. The more we do this, the easier it becomes.

Are there students in your classroom who might also like to do this? Sometimes we have students who are quite good at explaining how they go about the process of writing. It might be of benefit to writers to engage with their peers in this way.

Although many of the beautiful and powerful pieces my students wrote will never be seen by anyone other than those closest to them, the following are some examples of the essays that some students were willing to share. The following excerpt illustrates what Eduardo wrote about living on a dirt road and what it means to him, using the photo in Figure 12 as the basis for his essay.

> The street is something I have thought about all my life. When I was still a little child I thought the streets looked good. I used to live in a little house that had a dirt road in front of it. I was young but I wondered "How come everyone can live on a nice street and not me?" What I mean by "nice" is a street made of concrete with two sidewalks, one on either side. This bothered me. I lived in the city and yet I lived on a street made of dirt. After some time my family did move to a house on a concrete street which made me feel good....

Another student, Juan, wrote the following about the books that inspire, shape, and renew him, based on the photograph in Figure 13:

> These are my books. We don't own a big library, but I have always sought books that have a lesson to teach. You don't see the tears I've shed reading some of the books nor the things I've learned while reading them. You don't hear my laughter as I read the children's books. These books have contributed a lot to the making and the molding of me. I've learned some valuable lessons about life from these books. I've learned to smile, to laugh, to appreciate the simple things. I've learned to embrace solitude. I've learned it's good to be serious at times, but it's more important to kick your feet up and laugh sometimes.

Figure 12
Photo Accompanying Eduardo's Essay About Living on a Dirt Road

Figure 13
Photo Accompanying Juan's Essay on Books and Their Influence on His Life

Conclusion

At the beginning of this chapter I wrote about a photograph of myself lying on a bench with a copy of one of my beloved books held close to my heart. As I wrote I explored the way that books and objects define and represent who I am. Places and things and photographs of such can serve as symbols of ourselves. We can then use the physical realia and images, the symbolic representations of ourselves, to further explore and understand our identities through writing.

In the preface to her book about the artist Joseph Cornell, Ashton (1974) writes about how Cornell was defined and about how his work crystallized in his house on Utopia Parkway:

> In this shelter each fragment, whether a china squirrel, a ship's model, wood beads, or trifles from the sea, was significant to him. The poetic enactments which are his boxes and collages are the visible of this palace of dreams and associations. (p. 1)

When we help our students to use images and writing to define themselves we help them to look inward. For students of this age range, looking inward is relevant and meaningful. It is something they are most likely already engaged in doing and an important step in their growth as human beings.

As we help our students link their experiences in writing memoir to this experience in using images and writing to explore themselves, we guide them to think in ways that are centered in self. As students read, generate ideas, and talk about the identity of others as exemplified in full-length texts and short stories, they begin to explore the connections and disconnections they have with characters. As they read what Sandra Cisneros has written in a chapter from *The House on Mango Street* titled "My Name," they then write about their own names. They create a photograph that links the image and the identity they perceive for themselves as they continue this exploration. When students create photo collages to represent written texts, they create a foundation for looking at themselves in the same way. They can use this foundation to help them create Photo-Life Maps or photo collages that represent themselves. Finally, students distill these explorations into single or multiple images and an essay in which they describe these symbols and the connections between symbol and self. When we help our students to explore themselves through images and writing, we honor them as individuals. We tell them that we respect the people they are and the people that they are becoming.

REFERENCES

Allen, J., & Labbo, L. (2001). Giving it a second thought: Making culturally engaged teaching culturally engaging. *Language Arts, 79*, 40–52.

Ashton, D. (1974). *A Joseph Cornell album*. New York: Viking Press.

Isherwood, S., & Stanley, N. (Eds.). (1994). *Creating vision: Photography and the National Curriculum*. Manchester, England: Cornerhouse Publications.

Taylor, E.W. (2002). Using still photography in making meaning of adult educators' teaching beliefs. *Studies in the Education of Adults, 34*, 123–139.

Urdanivia-English, C. (2001). Whose history? Social studies in an elementary English class for speakers of other languages. *Social Studies, 92*, 193–197.

Van Horn, L. (2001). *Creating literacy communities in the middle school*. Norwood, MA: Christopher-Gordon.

LITERATURE CITED

Bambara, T.C. (1992). *Gorilla, my love*. New York: Vintage Contemporaries.

Buzzeo, T. (2002). *The sea chest*. New York: Dial Books for Young Readers.

Cisneros, S. (1984). *The house on Mango Street*. New York: Random House.

Fleischman, P. (1997). *Seedfolks*. New York: HarperCollins.

Franco, B. (Ed.). (2001). *Things I have to tell you: Poems and writing by teenage girls*. Cambridge, MA: Candlewick.

Gallo, D.R. (Ed.). (1984). *Sixteen short stories by outstanding writers for young adults*. New York: Delacorte.

Gallo, D.R. (Ed.). (1989). *Connections: Short stories by outstanding writers for young adults*. New York: Delacorte.

Giff, P.R. (2002). *Pictures of Hollis Woods*. New York: Random House.

Kendrick, R. (2005). *Revealing character: Texas tintypes*. Albany, TX: Bright Sky Press.

MacLachlan, P. (1991). *Journey*. New York: Delacorte.

Polacco, P. (2002). *When lightning comes in a jar*. New York: Philomel Books.

Rochman, H., & McCampbell, D.Z. (Eds.). (1993). *Who do you think you are? Stories of friends and enemies*. Boston: Little, Brown.

Solomon, B.H., & Panetta, E. (Eds.). (2004). *Once upon a childhood: Stories and memoirs of American youth*. New York: New American Library.

Soto, G. (1990). *Baseball in April and other stories*. New York: Harcourt Brace.

Walker, R. (2001). *Black, white, and Jewish: Autobiography of the shifting self*. New York: Riverhead Books.

CHAPTER 3

Creating Biographies With Voice: Reading Photographs to Write About People

A BROWN GROCERY BAG is a crisp, crackling weight against her hip. She loosely holds on to the worn leather purse that carried little but a lipstick, tissues to wipe runny noses, scratched dime-store sunglasses, and a compact with a chipped mirror inside. She has a scarf tied around her hair. She had just run to the store—she wasn't ready to have her picture taken. A few months ago they'd packed up the boys, bought a trailer, and moved to Texas City. They'd parked the trailer out under some scraggly tallow trees at the edge of the refinery. Every day she walked to the Cash and Carry. Inside, she stood real still and thought about the cardboard picture frames hanging in the window. She thought about buying one so she could stand her wedding picture up on the dresser—a foolhardy thought. That wedding in Arkansas was a long time ago...she was a Texas City woman now. Learning how to dream new dreams.

On the back of the photograph my mother-in-law, Dorothy, has written, "The grocery man where I trade made this." As I write about the photograph, I change this and pretend that my father-in-law is taking the picture. I think about what I know about Dorothy and Therman and examine the photograph for telling details. Then I imagine what she might be doing and thinking in these few moments. Later, as I read what I have written, I realize that the voice I hear is primarily my voice. However, if she were here today, she could tell me about this moment in her own words.

Our students seem to be fascinated by the lives of others. Some enjoy watching "reality" television shows; others may read the tabloids chronicling the lives of the stars in music, film, and sports. Still others like to sit on benches outside the school or in the hallways and watch the interactions of their peers. By engaging our students in reading and writing biographies and oral histories, we can help them develop this natural curiosity about people into a framework for looking at events and lives. We can begin to think about what makes each of us unique. We can identify connections between people and connections between events in an individual's life. A study of biography and writing biographies enables us to expand this interest in people to include those who have lived before our time and those who are living now.

There are many stories that need to be told. As we engage our students in a study of photographs to help them write biographies, we will be searching for individuals who have stories to tell us and wisdom to pass on. However, a biography should be more than a chronicle of events in a person's life—a powerful and meaningful biography will also capture the person's voice, allowing the reader to "see" and "hear" the individual as if you were sitting together, having a conversation. Therefore, we will also be listening to their voices and working to preserve the stories they tell us in the way that they tell them.

In addition, the experiences in this chapter address critical literacy and questions of identity. The activities in this chapter will enable students to develop an understanding of multiple perspectives, dialects, and ways of knowing that will be important to students as they read, listen to, and then write the stories of others' lives. Further, Daisey and Jose-Kampfner (2002) reveal that a study of biography helps students understand alternate possibilities and imagine new paths for their own lives as well. As you read about the processes involved in biography writing and the activities described in this chapter, it will be important for you to know how you might work with your students to develop your own definitions of critical literacy, identity, cultural practices, and agency.

Lewison, Flint, and Van Sluys (2002; p. 382) review definitions of critical literacy from the literature over the last 30 years to identify the following four dimensions of critical literacy:

1. Disrupting the commonplace

2. Interrogating multiple viewpoints

3. Focusing on sociopolitical issues

4. Taking action and promoting social justice.

As students engage in the learning experiences described in this chapter, they will be engaging in three of these four elements of critical literacy as they can be constructed or extracted from a study of oral history and biography writing. For example, students will "disrupt the commonplace" as they conduct the interviews that will compose the oral histories. As they look for individuals who have stories to tell and as they listen to and record these stories, students' personal perspective and viewpoint of history and historical events may be disrupted. Students will "interrogate multiple viewpoints" as they conduct photo and text analyses and then subsequently as they construct dialogue poems that represent a compilation of views on a single topic or event. Students will "focus on sociopolitical issues" when they gather data and write biographies focused on major events and primary-source documents chronicling the lives of people in their families or in their communities. Finally, although students may not take direct action or promote social justice at this point, they will be cognizant of the ways and means of gathering information in preparation for doing so.

Comber and Simpson (2001) state that "there is not one generic critical literacy, in theory or in practice. Rather there is a range of theories that are productive starting points for educators working on social justice issues through the literacy curriculum" (p. x). They remind us that "each group of students' specific cultural and political histories impact what is needed and what is possible" (p. x). Luke (2000; p. 453) describes the intended environment in a classroom devoted to critical literacy as one where students and teachers

> (a) see how the worlds of texts work to construct their worlds, their cultures, and their identities in powerful, often overtly ideological ways; and
> (b) use texts as social tools in ways that allow for a reconstruction of those same worlds.

As students investigate photographs, biography, voice, and oral history, they have an opportunity to note and "interrogate" multiple viewpoints, and this, in turn, enables them to exercise their linguistic resources (Stein, 2001). As students study their own voices and the voices of others, you can teach them to acknowledge and respect differing first languages, dialect, and ways of knowing. Stein (2001) writes of working with adolescents in South African schools in a multilingual storytelling project. She invited students to think of stories from their family or community that they would like to share out loud. The students were asked to work in groups where all in the group spoke the same language. Each person would tell a story in the language in which it was told to them. In whole-class presentations each group shared its best stories. Finally, the listeners commented on the stories and asked questions. As Stein reflects, "What began as a project intending to focus the uses of multilingualism in storytelling practices unexpectedly turned into an important project in the reappropriation and transformation of textual, cultural, and linguistic forms" (p. 151). The students in this example had opportunities to unearth family and community stories and to retell or reappropriate and transform them while preserving the essence of the original story and the voice of the person who told them the story. This experience illustrates how students might begin to learn how to preserve the voices and stories of others in a biography while working with a retelling of a well-known family or community story. With this in mind, we must work with our students to design experiences that will help them become aware of primary sources, voice, and the histories of people.

In this chapter we will examine and reflect upon ways that we can use photographs to help our students grapple with critical literacy, examine identity, and tell the life stories of people who are important by having students participate in the following authentic, meaningful activities:

- Examine photos and engage in a discussion about understanding individuals' stories and voices
- Analyze and write about the text and photographs of people in informational books to simulate the decision-making process of biographers and write a dialogue poem
- Choose a photograph from the Library of Congress website and write a biographical prose poem
- Search for the most important facts and details in informational texts and use this information to write and perform an Important Poem
- Read excerpts from primary-source documents to develop an understanding of voice
- Conduct an oral history interview
- Write a biography about a person in the community using *Martin's Big Words: The Life of Dr. Martin King, Jr.* (Rappaport, 2001) as the frame

ACTIVITY **1**

Introducing Students to the Concept of Voice

In order to get your students thinking about how biographies preserve the voice of the person they are written about, you may want to begin by having students examine a photograph from the past and try to use the content, person, and details in the photograph; the expressions on the faces of the people in the photograph; and the background in the photograph to help them understand more about the time and the person(s) depicted in the photograph (as I did in the opening vignette for this chapter). By doing this, students use visual images to help them make connections to people and places. This will help students to begin imagining themselves as collectors of stories. By engaging them in examining photographs, letters, postcards, and diaries, you can help them discover the means to preserve the stories of people through biography. You can also have students talk to people close to them and then invite them to tell the stories they might have about what it was like to live in a different community, time, or place, or what it was like to live during the time of a historical event, such as the Hurricane Katrina evacuation of New Orleans in 2005.

Ask your students to think about people they know and statements these individuals have made during particular events or times in their lives, statements that are particularly definitive of that person. When I do this with my students, we sit in a circle, and as people recall the moments in their lives when they have heard words that were full of the voice of the speaker, I quietly write the words and phrases on the board behind us. For example, in one class, I started us off by recalling that when things were difficult, my mother used to encourage us by saying, "In time, this too shall pass." When I shared that with my students the ideas began to flow. We heard about a grandmother who tries to make her granddaughter realize the wisdom she has because she has lived through a multitude of experiences, saying, "I've been your age—you've never been mine!" We heard about a grandfather who dismisses his grandson's fear or reluctance to act with the words, "Oh pshaw!" We listened as Ida told us about the way her mother reminds her that caring for and honoring her family and being true to herself are the things that matter most. Ida said that whenever she loses focus or finds herself wondering what she should do or how she should act in a situation, her mother urges her to "remember where you came from." One way you can capture your class's discussion and help students continue to reflect is to have students write the words and phrases on sentence strips and use them to create a word wall of statements that express individual voice.

As students listen to individuals talk about their lives and what matters to them, they develop an awareness of different life perspectives and views. They begin to attune themselves to the unique ways that individuals express themselves. They begin to hear the "voice" that is expressed in talk and to think about how to convey that voice on paper.

REFLECTION POINT

In what other ways can you introduce your students to the individual voice that is expressed in conversation?

Thinking Like a Biographer: Examining Photographs and Descriptive Text to Write Dialogue Poems

Do people who write biographies about others write about every aspect of the person's life? Some biographies focus on a particular aspect of a person's life or career. Then how do you decide what to include and what to leave out? To help students make these decisions, you can take them through a simulated process of how a biographer might make decisions to use photographs of people included in informational texts. Before working with students, first select books or other documents that include photographs of people and text that describes or explains something about the person and the time period. Then, after selecting the texts you will use, mark with sticky notes the excerpts of text and accompanying photos that you want students to read, noting the paragraphs and pages to be read by the students. See Table 5 for a list of recommended texts to use for this learning experience.

Begin by asking students to examine the photograph without looking at the accompanying text. You may want to do this as a whole class before asking students to do it on their own. You can make a transparency of the photograph to use with an overhead projector or you may project the photograph onto a screen using a digital projection device. Invite the students to examine the photograph and describe what they see, and create a list of all the details that students notice. After you demonstrate the process using a single photograph and soliciting student observations to create a whole-class list, students may then move to work in small groups to examine other photographs and create their own lists. Each group may use a different text with the photographs and excerpts marked with sticky notes if you can locate enough

Table 5
Suggested Literature Used to Simulate Biographer's Decision-Making Process

Appelt, K., & Schmitzer, J.C. (2001). *Down Cut Shin Creek: The pack horse librarians of Kentucky.* New York: HarperCollins.
Bolotin, N., & Herb, A. (1995). *For home and country: A Civil War scrapbook.* New York: Scholastic.
Freedman, R. (1980). *Immigrant kids.* New York: Dutton.
Gates, H.L., & West, C. (2000). *The African American century. How black Americans have shaped our country.* New York: The Free Press.
Granfield, L. (2000). *Pier 21: Gateway of hope.* Toronto, ON: Tundra.
Levine, K. (2002). *Hana's suitcase: A true story.* Morton Grove, IL: Albert Whitman.

different photographs and texts for each of the small groups. Each group can work with a photograph and then share with the other groups. For example, Sylvan and his group examined a photograph from *Down Cut Shin Creek: The Pack Horse Librarians of Kentucky* (Appelt & Schmitzer, 2001). Sylvan recorded the following for his group:

> It's an old picture. She's wearing a long skirt. The woman is on a horse and there are trees with no leaves so it must be winter. There are books in her hand. There is a sense of seriousness on her face like she knows what she is doing is important.

Next, invite students to read the text excerpt accompanying the photo and highlight or mark important facts and details with sticky notes, adding facts and details to their previous lists. As students do this, they can begin to see how a biographer might take note of important facts and details about an individual.

Next, have students reread the excerpt from the text and highlight or mark with sticky notes of a *different* color places where meaningful statements are made by the person in the photograph, adding these meaningful statements to the list. Students may also mark places where they feel that the person might have expressed himself or herself even though it is not written in the text. With these exercises we are preparing students to search for both important facts about a person and important statements made by the person when they write biography. For some students it may be simpler to mark both the important facts and details and important statements during the initial reading of the text. For example, Tenesha's group read excerpts and looked at photographs from *Hana's Suitcase: A True Story* (Levine, 2002). They marked the following facts with yellow sticky notes:

- "...Brady family's life was changed forever...." (p. 22)
- "...different rules...." (p. 22)
- "No Jews on the playground...gym...skating pond...." (p. 23)

Her group then marked with pink sticky notes the statements they felt are expressions of how Hana and her brother feel:

- "We'll be together forever, no matter what...." (p. 24)
- "It's not fair. I want it to be like it was before." (p. 25)
- "Maybe if we write down all the things that are bothering us it'll help us feel better." (p. 25)

Finally, ask your students to return to the photograph, examine it again, and consult the list of observations, facts, details, and meaningful statements recorded to create a dialogue poem. You may want to have students work individually to create their dialogue poems. I think of a dialogue poem as a series of statements people might have made, written in the form of conversational, back-and-forth dialogue. This dialogue poem will reflect the "voice" of the person or persons in the photograph and will build and expand upon what was read and observed in the text excerpt. For example, Tenesha's group examined a photograph of Hana and her mother hanging the wash on the line. They stand side by side with only the wooden laundry bucket between them. Both are wearing aprons over their dresses. Both are turned slightly toward one another and looking out at the camera. Behind the wash-line are bare trees and a house. Tenesha wrote,

It's not fair Mama. I want it to be like it was before...	Hush Hana. You know it cannot be. There are different rules now...
I don't want things to be different....	Hand me a clothes pin Hana. There's a dear.
I want to go to school....	Remember Hana. No matter what happens...
I want to play with Maria.	We'll be together forever.
I love you Mama...always.	If only in our thoughts.

REFLECTION POINT

Try this exercise for yourself—locate a biography with a photograph and accompanying text and create a dialogue poem based on any observations, details, facts, or statements you read in the text.

ACTIVITY 3

Noticing the Details: Writing Biographical Prose Poems

To expand upon the previous experience and to get your students to pay closer attention to biographical details, invite them to search the Library of Congress website for photographs they can use as a stimulus for writing. Begin by visiting the Library of Congress Prints and Photographs Online Catalog at www.loc.gov/rr/print/catalog.html. This will take you to a page that describes the catalog and how the photographs may be used. Many of these photographs may be downloaded and printed. Students may read about copyright and other use restrictions and then click on "search the catalog" to begin viewing photographs. These photographs can be used by the students as subjects for what Tom Romano (2000) defines as prose poems. He cites Oliver (1994), who describes the poems as "a fairly short block of type...looks like prose...often pure description...seems to have at its center a situation rather than a narrative...the syntax is often particularly exquisite" (pp. 86–87). This piece of writing differs from the dialogue poem previously described, because the focus of the prose poem is on vivid and clear description of the elements in the photograph and, if possible, a reflection on the possible emotions or feelings of the individual in the photograph.

You can use Oliver's definition to help plan how you can help our students write biographical prose poems. At the center of the prose poem is description. Depending upon the level of experience your students have with writing descriptive pieces, you may want to engage them in some "building" activities before they work on their own.

For example, I like to help my students attune themselves to descriptive language with a read-aloud of Karen Hesse's (1999) picture book *Come on Rain!* When I read the first few pages, I pause at places where I feel that Hesse is particularly descriptive (there are many such places throughout this book). I may read about how a woman bends over "parched plants" (p. 2) in the summer heat, or how the "smell of garbage bullies the air" (p. 7). After the first few pages, I slow my reading and invite the students to write in their writer's journals the descriptive words and phrases they hear. When we finish the book, I invite them to share what they've written. We create a list of phrases that includes describing a longing for rain as "a creeper of hope circles 'round my bones" (p. 4) and rain that "freckles our feet and glazes our toes" (p. 16). Next, students work with partners to examine other picture books or young adult novels for descriptive words and phrases that cause them to take notice. We refine our search to look for descriptions like "whipped cream clouds" rather than "fluffy clouds" and for "steamy, rain-soaked pavement" rather than "wet streets."

Depending upon the needs of your students, you may want to have them rework a piece they have in a draft stage, circling bland descriptions and replacing them with memorable ones. To show the impact of such changes, you can invite students to write their original phrase or sentence on the board and then place the revised piece underneath. When you have engaged in one or more of these experiences and feel that your students are ready to begin working independently, you may ask them to choose a photograph and begin writing their prose poems. It will be helpful to have students begin the process by creating a list of all the details in the photograph. They can then decide how they want to sequence the description (i.e., top to bottom, most important to least important, and so on). Finally, students might want to examine word banks, vividly written literature, and dictionaries to help them use powerful writing to describe the photograph.

For example, the photograph in Figure 14 depicts an unidentified African American woman (Library of Congress, n.d.). After downloading and printing this photograph, one of my students, Maria, wrote,

Figure 14

Photo of Unidentified Woman From U.S. Library of Congress Prints and Photographs Online Catalog

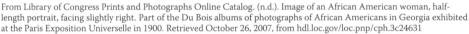

From Library of Congress Prints and Photographs Online Catalog. (n.d.). Image of an African American woman, half-length portrait, facing slightly right. Part of the Du Bois albums of photographs of African Americans in Georgia exhibited at the Paris Exposition Universelle in 1900. Retrieved October 26, 2007, from hdl.loc.gov/loc.pnp/cph.3c24631

Hair pomaded smooth from a center part. Head straight, she looks off into the distance as she settles herself and waits for the photographer to load the plate in his camera. Wanting to look more grown up than she feels, she wills herself to remain unsmiling. Warm in the crackling starched, pleated front cotton shirt. Twenty mother-of-pearl buttons to fasten it. The tightly cinched leather belt around her tiny waist makes her slightly short of breath. A vanity that comes with a cost. Heavy-lidded eyes, her glance is unflinching. She is resigned; expects little of any but herself. Ready...

FLASH! It is done.

REFLECTION POINT

Where else can your students find images they can work from? You may want to create a list of websites with a brief statement about each one so your students have a starting point where they can search for appropriate photographs. You may also want to choose an image and prepare for a "live" writing demonstration with your students.

Focusing on the Most Important Details:
Writing Important Poems

A biographer may conduct years of research before writing a book. As biographers conduct research in order to write about people, they must know what to include and what to leave out. As a writer sifts through informational texts, diaries, letters, and so on, it is important that he or she be able to locate and take away the information that will be used in the final piece. Likewise, your students may need to develop their ability to glean important facts and details from text. I have found that it is helpful and stimulating for students to practice this skill within the context of writing a poem for performance. I call these poems Important Poems, for they focus on what is important about an individual. The example that follows illustrates how to search for what is important about a person who lived or who is living.

Begin with a read-aloud of a poem or two from *The Important Book* (Brown, 1949). Ask students to listen as you read and to help identify the format the author is using. Brown writes of ordinary objects such as spoons, daisies, and grass. Through the writing she helps us see what is important and what is *most* important about each thing. You can write your own poem in the style of those in Brown's book, or you can have your students read the poems in *The Important Book* aloud. Through guided discussion, you can help them identify the format used by Brown. The following poem I wrote about a balloon imitates the style of those found in *The Important Book* and similarly focuses on what is most important about a balloon:

> The important thing about a balloon is that it makes you happy.
> It comes in many colors.
> It is made out of thin rubber.
> It has air or helium inside it to fill it out.
> The end of the balloon is knotted so what is inside will not escape.
> You have to tie a string on the end and hold on tight so you won't lose the balloon.
> But the important thing about a balloon is that it makes you happy.

As you can see the first and last line of the poem repeat what the author perceives to be the most important characteristic of the entity. In between there are always six statements about other important characteristics. When you have read a poem or two to your students, you can ask them to talk about what they are noticing about the format of the poem. Write down these observations so all can refer to them during the reading and writing process that follows.

Begin by giving students one- or two-page biographical information pieces about people you'd like your students to write about. For example, with my students I use pieces from the book *Scholastic Encyclopedia of Women in the United States* (Keenan, 1996). Have students work in pairs to read and talk about each excerpt and instruct them to work with a partner to take notes on what they think are the most important characteristics about the individual. Ask them not to copy statements directly from the text but to think about what they are reading and put it in their own words—otherwise, this becomes an exercise in copying text rather than one of reading and understanding. Once they have taken notes, instruct them to work with their partner to write an Important Poem using the format in *The Important Book*. In addition to the format derived from Brown's book, have students conclude with a statement made by the person or about the person that they feel represents the individual.

When the poems have been completed, have students copy the poems with permanent markers onto transparencies. Then ask the student partners to decide how they will perform the poem. Some may read in unison. Others will divide up the lines of the poem to be read alternately. Still others will create movement and/or sound to go along with the reading of the poem. The following is an example of an Important Poem about Toni Morrison written by two of my students, Kate and Tamara:

> The important thing about Toni Morrison is that she is a writer.
> She is an African-American woman who grew up during the era of the
> Great Depression.
> Stories she heard about inequality and injustice while growing up became
> her inspiration for writing.
> She searched for identity in the Bluest Eye...
> Wrote history in the Black Book...
> Won the 1988 Pulitzer Prize with Beloved.
> In 1993 she became the first African-American woman to win the
> Nobel Prize for literature.
> But the important thing about Toni Morrison is that she is a writer.
>
> "Writing is discovery; it's talking deep within myself." (Kate and Tamara included a quotation attributed to Toni Morrison to complete their poem. Quote from Keenan, S. [1996]. *Scholastic encyclopedia of women in the United States* [p. 184]. New York: Scholastic.)

After each reading, celebrate, talk about the writer's process, and note what students have learned about the featured individual. Writing both the prose poem and the Important Poem helps students attend to description, main idea, and summarization within creative experiences that include a number of reading/language arts skills. For example, students who create and perform a prose poem or an Important Poem may engage in viewing, thinking, writing, reading, and performing.

How can you design experiences that reinforce vital literacy skills within authentic creative opportunities for your students?

ACTIVITY 5

Understanding the Importance of Voice: Searching Primary-Source Documents

When you think of voice, you think of the statements people make or the words they write that reveal the unique individual qualities that make them who they are. History is often best told through the voices of the people who have lived or are living the events. Author Doreen Rappaport (2001) lets us "hear" the voice of Dr. Martin Luther King, Jr. in *Martin's Big Words: The Life of Dr. Martin Luther King, Jr.* But how do biographers help us come to know the people they write about?

Luckily, there is a great deal of material readily available that you can use to help your students explore the concept of voice. As you read primary-source documents, you "hear" the voices of many. When you work with your students who are reading primary-source documents to explore this concept, you will want to have them read to infer as much as possible about the writer, his or her circumstances, and the time and place in which he or she lives. To accomplish this, it may be helpful to engage your students in specific exercises focused on the strategy of "inferencing." For example, as students begin to make these inferences, they can use their writer's journals to record their developing ideas about the writer and his or her circumstances. Students should copy into their writer's journals excerpts from the text where they feel that they can "hear" the voice of the writer. You may want to have students work in small groups or with a partner to read aloud specific examples from their primary-source documents that illustrate voice. Another example is to work with your students to create a "voice" word wall with phrases or sentences the students have discovered in their readings that exemplify unique sentence structure or wording/voice.

In the next sections you will read about finding voice in the diaries, letters, and journals of people from the past; in historical documents such as treaties, pamphlets, and constitutions; in the students' own journals; and even in old postcards. Much of this material is available to our students in local libraries, through historical societies, or on the Internet. The activities I describe in the upcoming sections may be used with these primary-source documents as well. A study of the voices found in primary-source documents inspires biography writing.

Beginning With Published Primary-Source Documents

Begin by having your students examine various excerpts from published primary-source documents such as letters, diaries, and reports. This search may be conducted in the library, in the classroom, or on the Internet, or this search may be for realia or artifacts. I often begin by having my students read excerpts from *America's History Through Young Voices: Using Primary Sources in the K–12 Social Studies Classroom* (Wyman, 2005). My students and I read from a collection of letters written to Mrs. Roosevelt during the U.S. Great Depression. These letters evoke the trying conditions of life during this time. They often contain hopeful pleas to someone the writers truly believe can help. For example, Miss A.M. writes,

> I was just wondering, if you could do something, so I can graduate from the Eight grade. It will take about $10.00 and then I got to make my confirmation... I hope mother or dad wont find out I am writing to you, because they don't want to let anyone know how hard-up we are...I heard you help poor peoples. (pp. 130–131)

Other books that may serve as resources are *Documents of Texas History* (Wallace, Vigness, & Ward, 2002) and *Imagine: The Spirit of 20th-Century American Heroes* (Misiroglu, 1999). There is also an excellent collection of letters, excerpts from diaries and journals, and other primary-source material on the Library of Congress website at memory.loc.gov/ammem/browse/ListSome.php?category=Women's%20History. While searching the "Women in History" portion of the site, I found several noteworthy items, including printable images of a letter from Margaret Mead (Words and deeds, n.d.) explaining why she wanted to retain her maiden name after marriage, a character sketch of Amelia Earhart (Words and deeds, n.d.) made from impressions of her hands, and a letter from Eleanor Roosevelt to a Mr. White describing actions that could be taken to stop the practice of lynching in the south (Words and deeds, n.d.).

Examining Oral Histories

An oral history is a record or transcript of what a person said about an event or events. The person speaking often chooses the topic, but questions may be asked to help them begin. Oral history interviews literally capture voice as the interviewer records and writes exactly what is said by the individual being interviewed.

You might want to begin by listening to some of the StoryCorps interviews on National Public Radio. StoryCorps is a national project that builds upon the oral history interviews of Americans conducted during the 1930s. Participants choose someone to interview and the staff helps them design questions and record the interview in a soundproof recording booth. Participants receive a copy of the interview on CD, and the interview is archived in the StoryCorps Archive in the American Folklife Center at the Library of Congress. The first recording booth opened in New York City in October 2003. At present there are three stationary booths and two traveling booths called MobileBooths. You can find out more about the StoryCorps project by accessing www.storycorps.net/about/.

You may also access the Library of Congress website to read excerpts from other interviews that have been conducted and archived at memory.loc.gov. For example, in an exploration of the U.S. Great Depression, on the "Voices from the Thirties" homepage (memory.loc.gov/ammem/wpaintro/exhome .html), I was able to read excerpts from interviews on topics such as "All in a Day's Work: Industrial Lore," "Rank and File," "Hard Times in the City: Testifying," and "Making Do: Women and Work."

In another example, Ralph Ellison (1939) interviewed a man in a park in New York City and asked him, "Do rich people and poor people have anything in common?" The man answered,

> God made all this, and he made it for everybody. And he made it equal. This breeze and these green leaves out here is for everybody. The same sun's shining down on everybody. This breeze comes from God and man cain't do nothing about it. I breath the same air old man Ford and old man Rockefeller breath. They got all the money and I ain't got nothing, but they got to breath the same air I do. (memory.loc.gov/ammem/wpaintro/man park.html)

Clyde "Kingfish" Smith, a street vendor in Harlem, New York City, talked to Marion Charles Hatch (1939) about why he started singing while he worked. He said,

> When I started peddling that was in 1932, that's when I started singing...'Heighho, fish man, bring down you dishpan,' that's what started it. Fish ain't but five cent a pound. It was hard times then, the Depression, and people can hardly believe fish is five cents a pound, so they started buying. There was quite a few peddlers and somebody had to have something extra to attract the attention. (memory.loc.gov/ammem/wpaintro/clyde.html)

As students search out and read these interviews you may want to have them share pieces aloud that they feel are particularly good examples of the unique aspects of voice. It is through the reading and the sharing of these interviews that students will develop ideas about how our voices individualize us. As they come to this understanding they will also realize how important it will be for them to preserve the voices of their subjects in the pieces they will write.

Looking for Voice in Old Postcards

Examples of voice are all around us. Several months ago while I was wandering through a secondhand or "antique" shop, I took notice of a basket full of old postcards. Postcard writing is a unique genre. When someone writes a postcard, they write in limited space and they write a message that anyone other than the addressee may read. Postcards are written in haste, often as one travels far from home. The voices of the writers of postcards are somewhat urgent; they do not take the time to ponder flowery words or long, drawn-out explanations. When we write postcards, we record our strongest impressions of a place or an event; we report back to those we have left behind.

Invite your students to consider the different voices they "hear" in a handful of postcards. Is it possible to tell whether people from different places express themselves in different ways? An examination of a handful of postcards will help our students gather ideas about what others deem most important. As a genre, postcards are breezy, somewhat breathless reports of what is most important to the writer. Writers often choose a postcard with a photograph that represents an important moment or theme of the journey. Writers often inquire about the addressee at the beginning or end of the card. They make short, succinct statements about what they are doing and seeing. Weather and time are frequent topics. Within all of the standard elements, you can sense the persona of the writer through the choice and positioning of words and phrases.

With this in mind, begin by collecting old postcards, or invite your students to share with the class any they have at home. Copies can be made of postcards that need to be returned. Keep in mind that writers of postcards often try to fit as much as possible into a small space, so attempt to choose cards that students will be able to decipher. Select a postcard to share with the class and model how students can read and examine postcards to hear the writer's voice.

For example, a postcard containing a picture of a group of people lining the rim of a canyon on Kaui, Hawaii, USA, and addressed to someone in Texas, USA, reads,

Aloha!

Can you find me in the line of spectators?

I remember when you took me to Kaui while you were visiting with us in Honolulu!

Thanks again!

Enjoyed seeing many of our old friends in Honolulu and, of course, the weather!

Love,

Me

As I shared the postcard with the class, we began attempting to determine the context in which it was written and, if possible, the relationship between the author and the addressee. In reading this postcard, we might surmise that the writer had at one time lived in Honolulu and that the person receiving the postcard had come to visit her and taken her on a day trip to visit Kaui. Now it seems that this person has grown and has returned to Honolulu for a short trip. While there, the writer has visited some of the people she knew when she lived there previously. During the second and third reading of the postcard, we identified places where we felt we could "hear" the voice of the author. Reading what this person has written, we could see that she is enthusiastic (the number of exclamation points) and that she appreciates friends and friendship (her remembrance of the trip she took with the person she is sending the postcard to, her enjoyment in seeing old friends again, and her closure with the word *love*).

In another example, a postcard depicts a towering skyscraper in New York City and is addressed to someone in Texas. It reads,

Got tickets to see "High Spirits" with Bea Lillie tonight. Tomorrow we go to the Fair—hope the weather clears up at least to a drizzle for us. Have you written me? I'd better find a letter when I get back! Tell Grandma, Grandpa, and D.A. "hi" for me.

Love,

Mother

As we read this postcard, we might suppose that the receiver of the postcard is the daughter of the author of the card. She may be living with her grandmother and grandfather. The author of the card, it seems, is taking a weekend trip to New York with someone, perhaps her husband. She writes of the activities she has planned for her visit and of the weather. Reading what she has written, we might say that she is organized (has an itinerary of activities) and that she is hopeful/optimistic about having a good time in New York ("hope the weather clears up at least to a drizzle..."). We might guess that she has not received a letter from her daughter in a while and that she feels comfortable enough with her to ask about it and to gently demand a letter with the words "I'd better find a letter when I get back!"

Similarly, students might work in pairs to study the image, read the message, and create a list of inferences they can make about the location depicted, the writer, and/or the person who received the postcard. As students engage in this process, they attune themselves to the various ways that people express themselves—the unique "voices" that we have. They also become more adept at making inferences.

Students Finding Their Voices in Their Own Journals

Another place students can look for voice is in their own writer's journals. To help students begin to recognize instances in their writing where their voice is apparent, ask them to spend a few moments rereading their journal entries. As they read they should ask themselves if what they are reading sounds like "me talking." For example, a student might choose a page from his journal where he was working with the idea of an internal monologue and writing his thoughts as they came to him one morning while he waited for the school bus. This might look like the following example:

> Aaaagh! I'm freezing. I can feel the oatmeal I ate jumping around inside me when I shake! When is that bus going to get here? Seems like it takes longer every day. Then when it does get here I've got to try to get a seat by someone I feel like talking to all the way to school. Maybe I won't talk. Maybe I'll just pretend like I'm sleeping. Maybe if I stamp my feet around I won't freeze and stick to the sidewalk. Oh, no! Would you look at that—I've got two different socks on. That's what I get for looking around in the dirty clothes basket for some socks. Should have turned the light on. I might have ended up with two blue socks instead of a blue one and a brown one. Wonder if anyone will notice? Can you go without socks when it's 50 degrees outside????

Reading this, we can hear the frustration in his voice. We can see how he worries about his relationships with his peers, his clothes, perhaps getting to school on time. We notice that he uses sarcasm or humor to recover.

You can prompt this kind of writing by asking students to discuss a "chain of thought" they have. For example, I might be loading my car for work. As I put in the shoes I'll wear to walk from the parking lot to my office, I might think about what I will see as I cross the bridge over the bayou. I might think about the funny-looking ducks I saw waddling along the bank of the bayou the other day. I might think about the time that Griselda, one of my students, stopped me on the bridge to show me the "giant fish" she saw swimming in the water. I'll remember how she told me her dad had a catfish that size in a tank at home and how she laughed when I asked her if they were going to eat it. These "chains of thought" reveal the way our minds work, the connections we make, and what we may think is important at the time.

Another student, Katie, shared a page from her journal, written while riding on a Greyhound bus back from a trip home to New York to visit an ailing father. Her father is sick, her relationship with her boyfriend is feeling one-sided, and she is reflecting on what she wants from life. She wrote,

> I want to fall madly in love with a person who makes me happy and do the same for him. I want to marry him on the beach, let the sand move between my toes with the ocean beating against the shore. I want to live near the beach, have a couple of children, become a teacher and have a classroom in which my students want to come to every day and LIVE LIFE!! I know it may sound like I want it all, but I feel that it is just happiness that I long for...that's it.

When writers have found an entry that exhibits their voice and one they are willing to share, have them set up what Calkins (1994) calls a "Notebook Museum" (p. 33). At each desk a notebook is laid open to a page that the writer is willing to have others read. I like to give each of my students a pack of sticky notes to take along with them. As they read they can leave a note expressing their thoughts, wonderings, and appreciation to the writer of the notebook. This experience gives us greater understanding and greater respect for the many different voices within our classroom. Having done this, you may want to expand upon the process by having an "exhibition" of historical documents, journals, letters, and diaries written by people from the past. Students could circulate among the pieces with their journals in hand, noting particular examples of voice and citing the document from which they came.

REFLECTION POINT

Do your students keep journals? If so, read through their journals and look for places where they are exercising their voices. Can you develop a minilesson using excerpts from their journals or from your own journal to show how different writers have different voices? Be sure to ask students if you can use excerpts from their journals to help you demonstrate this concept. Students are usually happy to have their work shared with others.

ACTIVITY **6**

Conducting Oral History Interviews

As you begin planning to conduct an oral history interview, one of the first questions always is "Who should we interview?" To help students think about interesting people they may know that they can interview, invite them to sit in a circle with you and "tell stories" about the people in their lives. I begin by telling my students about a man who lives across the street from me. He owns the lot next to his house, and he is building a house on that lot. I can look out my front windows and watch him, his wife, and his eldest son lifting up the plywood boards that will form the floor of the second story of their house. Later, as the sun sets, I see them sitting in plastic lounge chairs in the middle of the second story floor, looking at what they have accomplished that day. My neighbor has told me that his family is too big for the house they live in now, and when they finish building the new house, they will move into it and sell the first house. I think because he can build his own home that he would be an interesting person to interview.

By telling your own story first, you will likely get your students thinking about their own stories of interesting people they know. For instance, the story about my neighbor prompted one of my students, Garnet, to tell the class about an old "mom and pop" store in a stone building across from a dilapidated park. She said, "The woman in there knew my grandma. We stayed with her for a while. This woman would always give me candy. Or she would call out to the guy in back and tell him to bring up a pressed ham. He would cut it up for us." Garnet concluded with the statement, "A year ago I went back and she still remembers my grandma." A woman who has run a neighborhood store for all these years is likely to have a fascinating history to tell. Another student, Cherry, shared with the class the story of a man in her neighborhood, saying, "He has been a paraplegic since the age of 17...he's always lived in the same house in our neighborhood. I've always wanted to know more about him and his life." She looked up excitedly and asked herself, "I wonder if now would be a good time to find out?" We decided to think further and perhaps talk to the people we want to feature in our oral history interviews to see how they feel about being interviewed.

When you do this with your students, you may want to end the experience by allowing them time to jot down the story they shared in class. They can use these notes to prompt further thinking and, perhaps, share them with the person they want to interview. The sharing of the story in class and the recording of the story in notes demonstrates the students' interest in the individuals to be interviewed and in the project. If students choose to share their notes with potential interviewees, this could be an invitation for them to share related stories.

Conducting the Interviews and Taking Photographs of the Interviewee

When preparing to conduct an interview, there is often a temptation to create a lengthy list of questions. Interviewers feel safe when they have questions; they will not be at a loss for something to say. The problem with this is that an interview based on a list of questions created by the interviewer may be more about what the interviewer perceives as being important than about the person being interviewed. Therefore, develop a protocol for the oral history interviews. The protocol I developed for my classes consists of one or two open-ended questions and a few follow-up questions. The task I assign my students is to listen to the person being interviewed and to ask them questions that will help them expand upon what they are telling us.

Students may need to practice listening and responding skills so they will be able to respond appropriately during the interview process. For example, can students listen to what is being said and know when to stay silent and when and what to ask to encourage the individual to expand upon what he or she is saying? This is something you could practice in your classroom. You might have two students volunteer to conduct a mock interview in a "fishbowl" in the center of the room. Students who are watching the interview could interject with ideas and further questions during the mock interview, or their thoughts could be solicited following the interview.

Advise your students to audiotape their interviews. It is very difficult to give the interviewee your undivided attention, to make eye contact, to actively listen, and to formulate follow-up questions while you are trying to write down everything just as it is said to preserve voice. It is much simpler for students to audiotape the interviews and then play back the tape as they write the interview. Some schools may even have transcribing machines available (these are machines that enable the user to stop and rewind the recording with a foot pedal while listening to the interview through headphones and then writing).

In addition, before students begin interviewing, you will want to talk to them about taking photographs to accompany the interview. In the previous activities, students have been working with existing photographs, but for the oral history interview, students will take a photograph to accompany their interviews. "What if the person I'm interviewing doesn't feel comfortable being photographed?" a student might ask. If the interviewee does not want his or her photo taken, instead your students may take a photograph of something that represents the person or that represents the event that he or she recollects for the interview. For example, if a student interviews someone who talks about serving in the military, he or she might include a photograph of that person's hands holding a flag or of a flag flying in the breeze.

When students have transcribed their interviews and printed their photographs, they are ready to put the final touches on the product. Students will need to write an introduction for their interviews. They should begin with a description of the person being interviewed and the setting or context for the interview. The written interview can be presented in a binder or portfolio with the photograph of the interviewee or an object representing the interviewee on the cover.

Sharing the Interviews

Once the assignment is complete, have students read the oral history interviews aloud to one another as a class. Sharing their oral history interviews as a class will help students realize all that they accomplished. You can enhance the sharing and provide a dual focus on the process and the product by asking students to discuss how they formulated their questions, how they made their interviewee comfortable, how they encouraged him or her to extend and expand upon what they were saying, and so on. Students can also talk about how they transcribed the interview, preserving the specific words and dialect of the individual, and how they used photographs to represent the individual interviewed. When students cannot or do not photograph the interviewee, they can discuss how they decided upon a symbol to represent this person. This experience has enabled students to honor the individuals in their communities as they learned more about them. By sharing their stories, students will come to know stories of people who are survivors, dreamers, and planners, people who are making a difference. In addition, these oral histories can stand alone or become a part of a lengthier biography of a living individual. Also, students may be able to submit their oral history interviews to be included on the Library of Congress website (see www.loc.gov for more information).

One of my students, Martina, interviewed one of her teachers (see Figure 15 for the photo accompanying Martina's project). The teacher began the interview by telling the following story to Martina:

> Well, I started a long time ago when I was in Cuba. In Cuba we have what we call a magnet school for teachers, "Escuela Normal," and they were for young teachers that graduated from there and the government sends you to the fields, the rural areas, and you teach elementary there. That's what I was doing when Castro came in; I was a rural school teacher. I used to take two buses to get there and then walk on land to a little school three or four grades at the same time, multiple grades in one classroom setting. But at the same time I was earning my education degree. When Castro came they closed the university where I was and then my mother wanted to come to the United States so I came with them and at that time I was 21.

Another student, Todd, interviewed a prominent member of the local Vietnamese community (see Figure 16 for the photo accompanying Todd's project). He describes what it was like for him to travel to the United States in the following excerpt from the interview:

> I came to the U.S. in 1976 when I was 20. My family escaped the Vietnam communist in 1975. We were on a boat and in a night after three or four days on the ocean. The boat had

Figure 15
Photo Accompanying Martina's Oral History Interview of Teacher

a hole and water was coming in. The rain started to fall down. Everybody was cry and scary. Some of them tried to fix the hole and some people used cups or cans to get the water out of the boat. While doing that a man fell down the ocean. The captain on the boat jumped down the ocean to help the man get back on the boat. It was dark and the captain was tired. He couldn't swim anymore. The captain and the man died on the ocean. Everyone on the boat felt sorry for both of them. We fixed the hole and the rain stopped. We continued our trip on the boat without a captain. We floated on the ocean for a week. We finally ran out of water and food. We were so hungry we could not get up. We saw a big ship. People on the ship let us get on their ship and gave us food. They took us to Malaysia. We lived in a camp for two months.

REFLECTION POINT

The oral history project enabled us to document the stories of some of the members of our immediate community. How might you expand upon this experience? How could you save and build upon these documents to create an archive of stories from your community? Is there any way that students could refer to such an archive for later learning experiences? Think further about ways that you might make the most of this experience.

Figure 16
Photo Accompanying Todd's Oral History Interview of Local Community Member

Writing a Biographical Essay

One of the most unique biographies I have encountered is *Martin's Big Words: The Life of Dr. Martin Luther King, Jr.*, written by Doreen Rappaport (2001). This book is formatted so the top portion of a page includes details from Dr. King's life, while the bottom half of the page includes excerpts from his speeches or other statements. The illustrations on which the writing is superimposed or which face the writing on alternate pages are collages of painted and found images as well as photographs. The text is formatted in two different type sizes and colors: one color and type size depicts events in King's life, while the other reflects quotes from his speeches. The text at the beginning of each page tells us about the life of Dr. King. The larger text underneath lets us "hear" the voice of Dr. King. For example, Rappaport writes about the protest marches for equal rights in the South with the following words:

> White ministers told them to stop.
> Mayors and governors and police chiefs and judges
> ordered them to stop.
> But they kept on marching. (p. 13)

She then lets readers hear the words of Dr. King in response to these events in his life and the life of others with these words excerpted from one of his many public speeches:

> Wait! For years I have
> heard the word "Wait!"
> We have waited more than
> three hundred and forty years
> for our rights. (p. 10)

Read this book aloud with your students and use it as an introduction to the process of writing biography. Other biographies that also serve this purpose well are listed in Table 6. When I share this text with my students, I ask them to listen as I read it aloud and to look at the book closely. I ask them to let me know what they are noticing. Before too long someone will exclaim, "The big words are his words; they're the words we have heard him say or words he's written in his speeches." As we read on, someone else will stop me to say something like, "The big words deal with what's happening above them in the text—they tell us what he might have said at that time." We talk

---

Table 6
Texts to Inspire Biographical Writing

Younger Students
Fradin, J.B. (2004). *Power of one: Daisy Bates and the Little Rock nine*. New York: Clarion Books.
Friedman, C. (2005). *Nicky the jazz cat*. New York: PowerHouse Books.
Myers, W.D. (1996). *Brown angels: An album of pictures and verse*. New York: HarperCollins.
Taylor, D.A. (2004). *Sweet music in Harlem*. New York: Lee & Low.

Students in Grades 7 and Above
Alvarez, J. (1995). *In the time of the butterflies*. New York: Penguin.
Alvarez, J. (2004). *Before we were free*. New York: Knopf.
Hamilton, V. (2006). *The house of Dies Drear*. New York: Simon & Schuster.
Jiménez, F. (2002). *Breaking through*. Boston: Houghton Mifflin.
Kadohata, C. (2006). *Kira-Kira*. New York: Simon & Schuster.
Ryan, P.M. (2002). *Esperanza rising*. New York: Scholastic.
Yep, L. (1977). *Dragonwings*. New York: HarperCollins.

about how we can hear his voice in the big words and how that enriches the experience of the biography, the story of his life.

Because this unique biography format incorporates a variety of "ways of knowing" (i.e., recounting or retelling of several events), photographs that represent the individual and/or the event(s), and finally, writings created by the person that relate to the event, this text will be the model for the biography students will write. This activity will be broken down into three steps: writing about three main events of the person's life, collecting and writing about the documents of the person that relate to the events, and creating a photograph that represents the person and the events. The experiences described up to this point in the chapter will provide students with the information and background knowledge they need to create a biography of their own by using a format similar to that of *Martin's Big Words*.

REFLECTION POINT

Look on your shelves for biographies or autobiographies. Which ones do you think you would share with your students? Do you have biographies or autobiographies that have particular features you would like your students to use as models? Do you have books or pieces about people that would interest your students or reflect the culture of your students?

Biography Project Guidelines

Before students begin writing, you will want to create guidelines for the project with your students. As you talk about each aspect of the project, you will help students clarify what and how it will be done. You may want to take notes in a place where all students can see them as you construct the list that will become the guidelines for the project.

As with the oral history interviews, you will want to use a photograph or photographs as the initial inspiration for the piece. If a person a student wants to write about isn't alive or doesn't want to be photographed, it is perfectly acceptable for the student to instead include a photograph that is representative of the person, such as a picture of the place where he or she lives or lived, or a photograph of something that was important to him or her. As this discussion concludes, you might write, "Take a photograph of the person who is the subject of your biography or a picture of an object that represents something about the person." These photographs will take the place of the illustrations in *Martin's Big Words*.

You might want to think about the question of what part or parts of a person's life is included by a biographer. Doreen Rappaport did not include every event of Dr. King's life in her biography of him; she had to make choices. Because your students are going to be writing essays rather than full-length biographies, you might have students choose three meaningful moments in a person's life. If so, then you would add to your list "Write about three meaningful moments in the individual's life." You might note that student biographers do not have to have been present or to know the person during the moments or events that are the subject of the biography. For example, a student might interview his grandmother about an experience or series of events that occurred in her life before he was born. You would add this decision to your list.

Finally, in order to write a biography based upon the format used in *Martin's Big Words* you will need to include something that the subject of the biography said or wrote down in a diary, card, or letter that related to each of the three events. With this inclusion, we would be interpretively re-creating the portion of *Martin's Big Words* where Rappaport includes the words from the speeches of Dr. Martin Luther King, Jr. If you choose to include this step in your guidelines for the project, you will need to read and discuss the text with your students.

When you feel you have concluded your discussion, you can order this list to create guidelines for your students. Creating the guidelines in this way makes it a collaborative process and allows your students to talk about their concerns and questions. In many cases, this kind of discussion enriches the project as students may come up with ideas you have not considered. Guidelines such as these can also serve as rubrics for students. When you create the guidelines with your students, they help formulate and, as a result, internalize what is expected of them in terms of the process and successful completion of the project. Students may be given printed copies of the guidelines to use as they work on the project. They may also use the guidelines as a rubric to self-evaluate their work before turning it in to you.

Looking at Our Own Biographies Based Upon Martin's Big Words

Many of my students wrote about family members and based their writings upon photographs from family albums—you will likely find similar results in your classroom. These biographies became tributes to those they love and to the memorable moments that are often captured in family photographs. Because the photographs are irreplaceable and because they depict private moments, they are not included here. If you have scanners or high-resolution copy machines available to you in your school, you might want to reproduce your students' essays and photographs. You might create a class book or individual books that can be displayed in the school library. In this way the members of the community can be honored and known by all who read their stories.

Figure 17
Diana's Photo of Family Notebook for Biography Project

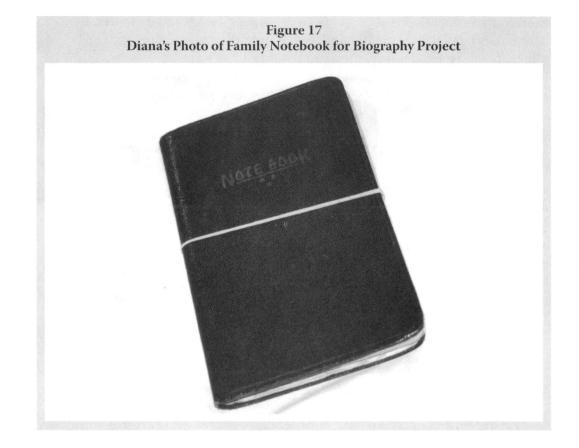

In my class, one of my students, Diana, wrote the following about her grandmother (see Figure 17 for the photo that accompanied her biography):

> My grandmother traveled with my grandfather who worked for the Magnolia Oil Company. At that time the workers followed the oil and most of the oil rigs were set up near railroad towns like Tomball, Sealy, Columbus, Beaumont, Nederland, Edna and Bishop...I happened upon this book shortly after my grandmother's funeral service. I felt that I was the only one in the family that would appreciate the value of the words penned in its pages.... It is held together by a rubber band because many of the pages are falling out. The oldest dated writing in the book is dated September 1939, Sealy, Texas. It says: "...You are ever ready to share joys and sorrows with those you meet. I wish you most happiness in your new home wherever you go...."

Another student, Lavinia, wrote about her mother, who has told her what it was like to travel across the country picking crops when she really wanted to be in school:

> It was my senior year in high school. Of course we didn't start on the first day of school. My family were migrant workers and we were headed northwest to Idaho in search of work. I remember one man asking me if I had ever been to school. His face reddened

when I said to him, "Hey, this is my senior year." Upon our return to our home town in November I had to register in school. I had no one to speak for me. I went to the vice-principal and asked if I could start school. His reply to me was "You don't need a diploma, you have work."

Conclusion

At the beginning of this chapter I wrote about a photograph of my mother-in-law standing in front of a grocery store. As I wrote, I tried to imagine what she was thinking and what she would say about this moment in her life. Later, when I read what I had written, I realized that the voice in my piece was mine rather than hers. I realized that I needed her voice to fully capture that moment. When we think about writing biographies with voice about people who exist today—those related to us or those who live and work in our communities—we recognize the opportunity we have to capture their voices as we record important details from their lives. We must learn to listen and to record the words and then to reflect upon the meaning behind the words. For the writers in our classrooms, this is similar to attending to the words in a text and then making meaning or interpreting the text.

Gordon S. Wood (2004), Pulitzer Prize–winning biographer of Benjamin Franklin, writes in the Preface of *The Americanization of Benjamin Franklin* that he has not written a traditional biography, rather that he has created a "selective study, focusing on specific aspects of this extraordinary man's life that reveal a Benjamin Franklin who is different in important ways from the Franklin of our inherited common understanding" (p. ix). Just as it was not his intent to write a traditional biography, it was not the intent of this chapter to talk about helping students write traditional biographies. When we help our students attend to voice, conduct interviews to create oral histories, and write biographies based upon three key events, and when we ask them to weave excerpts from diaries, journals, letters, and other sources related to these events into their biographies, we help them formulate new ideas about biography. When we do these things we help them shape and transform biographical writing so they can focus on the people in their community. We help them transform biographical writing so it becomes something they can do well with passion and creativity and in authentic ways.

These experiences help our students break down aspects of biographical writing and reshape them to focus on individuals close to them. When we think about the stories those close to us may tell, when we study how an individual's "voice" is heard in print text, when we consider what events in a life are most important and how these events relate to one another, we are creating biographies with voice about people we know. This is how the people of the future will know about the people who live today.

REFERENCES

Calkins, L.M. (1994). *The art of teaching writing* (New ed.). Portsmouth, NH: Heinemann.

Comber, B., & Simpson, A. (Eds.). (2001). *Negotiating critical literacies in classrooms.* Mahwah, NJ: Erlbaum.

Daisey, P., & Jose-Kampfner, C. (2002). The power of story to expand possible selves for Latina middle school students. *Journal of Adolescent & Adult Literacy, 45,* 578–587.

Ellison, R. (1939). *Man at Colonial Park.* Library of Congress, Manuscript Division, WPA Federal Writers' Project Collection. Retrieved June 1, 2006, from memory.loc.gov/ammem/wpaintro/manpark.html

Hatch, M.C. (1939). *Clyde "Kingfish" Smith, street vendor.* Library of Congress, Manuscript Division, WPA Federal Writers' Project Collection. Retrieved June 1, 2006, from memory.loc.gov/ammem/wpaintro/clyde.html

Lewison, M., Flint, A.S., & Van Sluys, K. (2002). Taking on critical literacy: The journey of newcomers and novices. *Language Arts, 79,* 382–392.

Library of Congress Prints and Photographs Online Catalog. (n.d.). Image of an African American woman, half-length portrait, facing slightly right. Part of the Du Bois albums of photographs of African Americans in Georgia exhibited at the Paris Exposition Universelle in 1900. Retrieved October 26, 2007, from hdl.loc.gov/loc.pnp/cph.3c24631

Luke, A. (2000). Critical literacy in Australia: A matter of context and standpoint. *Journal of Adolescent & Adult Literacy, 43,* 448–461.

Oliver, M. (1994). *A poetry handbook.* San Diego, CA: Harcourt.

Romano, T. (2000). *Blending genre, altering style: Writing multigenre papers.* Portsmouth, NH: Heinemann.

Stein, P. (2001). Classrooms as sites of textual, cultural, and linguistic reappropriation. In B. Comber & A. Simpson (Eds.), *Negotiating critical literacies in classrooms* (pp. 151–169). Mahwah, NJ: Erlbaum.

Wood, G.S. (2004). *The Americanization of Benjamin Franklin.* New York: Penguin Press.

Words and deeds in American history. (n.d.). Amelia Earhart's palm print and analysis of her character prepared by Nellie Simmons Meier, 1933. Retrieved June 1, 2006, from memory.loc.gov/cgi-bin/ampage?collId=mcc&fileName=038/page.db&recNum=0&itemLink=r?am

Words and deeds in American history. (n.d.). Image of a letter from Margaret Mead, 1923. Retrieved June 1, 2006, from memory.loc.gov/cgi-bin/ampage?collId=mcc&fileName=037/page.db&recNum=0&itemLink=r?am

Words and deeds in American history. (n.d.). Image of a letter from Mrs. Eleanor Roosevelt, 1936. Retrieved June 1, 2006, from memory.loc.gov/cgi-bin/ampage?collId=mcc&fileName=015/page.db&recNum=0&itemLink=r?am

LITERATURE CITED

Appelt, K., & Schmitzer, J.C. (2001). *Down Cut Shin Creek: The pack horse librarians of Kentucky.* New York: HarperCollins.

Brown, M.W. (1949). *The important book.* New York: HarperCollins.

Hesse, K. (1999). *Come on rain!* New York: Scholastic.

Keenan, S. (1996). *Scholastic encyclopedia of women in the United States.* New York: Scholastic.

Levine, K. (2002). *Hana's suitcase: A true story.* Morton Grove, IL: Albert Whitman.

Misiroglu, G. (Ed.). (1999). *Imagine: The spirit of 20th-century American heroes.* New York: MJF Books.

Rappaport, D. (2001). *Martin's big words: The life of Dr. Martin Luther King, Jr.* New York: Hyperion Books for Children.

Wallace, E., Vigness, D.M., & Ward, G.B. (2002). *Documents of Texas history* (2nd ed.). Austin: Texas State Historical Association.

Wyman, R.M., Jr. (2005). *America's history through young voices: Using primary sources in the K–12 social studies classroom.* Upper Saddle River, NJ: Pearson Education.

Discovering the Community: Reading Photographs to Write About Relevant Social Issues

WHAT DO I SEE in this photo? Around the edges of the photograph in a broken circle is a dark, blurry smudge. Just inside the smudge, on the right, the

front end of a 1943 Mercury angles into the center. It has glass headlights like watchful eyes, and its chromed grill is a straight-mouthed grin. Fastened to the formidable front bumper is a 1950 Illinois license plate, number 1472 447. On the left side of the photograph stand two metal trash cans, their lids in place. A pole that may be an electric pole or may be a clothesline is in the left foreground. In the center back of the photograph is the trunk of a creosoted telephone pole. In front of that is a metal trailer with rounded edges. The trailer is tricolored; a dark band around the bottom to the midpoint, a lighter band around the windows, and an even lighter band at the top of the trailer. The window on the front right side of the trailer is propped open. The trailer sits on a bed of gravel and light weeds. The screen door of the trailer is open and in front of the door, standing on a piece of 3/4–inch plywood, is Dorothy. She is wearing a short-sleeved, light-colored, belted cotton housedress with a bow at the peak of the v-neck. She has white crew socks and lace-up tennis shoes on her feet. Her head and body are turned slightly to the camera.

What might be happening here? This is Dorothy's trailer in Texas City. She may have been about to go inside to fix lunch. It looks as if there is a visitor from Illinois in the trailer park. Someone may have asked her to wait a minute to have her picture taken.

How might she feel at this moment? She is probably trying to be polite while feeling some impatience. She is probably hungry and anxious to make lunch and enjoy it in peace before she has to get started with the afternoon chores.

How would I feel if I were there? Lonely, I think I would feel lonely. I don't see anyone else around and it "feels" like a storm is brewing.

What do I wonder about this photo? I wonder what she was thinking. I wonder if she liked living here. I wonder what she did all day while the boys were at school and Therman was at work. I wonder if she had friends here. I wonder if she had a hobby. I wonder if she derived satisfaction from all that she did.

What surprises me? I am surprised at how small the trailer looks. So small to hold the lives of six people. They must have been so close.

My examination of this photograph of Dorothy in a community setting is guided by a set of specific questions. What do I see? What might be happening here? How might the person in the photograph feel? How would I feel if I were in the photograph? What do I wonder about the photograph? What surprises me? Yet as I examine the photograph in this way, I develop an understanding not only about Dorothy but also about the community in which she lives. This guided journey into the photograph enables me to think about an issue or issues of social relevance connected to the images depicted in the photograph.

For example, as I think about how she might feel and note that she lives in a trailer park, I might think about the conditions of living in the trailer park: Is there enough room or a place for children to play? Does she have friends there? Is there a library nearby? A grocery store? When I note that she is alone in what appears to be the middle of the day, I may think about whether she is a stay-at-home mother or a single mother. I might wonder about issues that would be important to her such as child care, schooling, recreation, and health care for her children. As you can see, my examination of the photograph is similar to our previous examinations in that I take stock of all the elements within the frame. However, the difference this time is that I am looking at the elements in the photograph with a specific focus on potential issues of social relevance.

It is critical for us to engage our students in experiences that demonstrate the potential for literacy to support positive activism. Through these classroom experiences, we hope to develop a heightened sense of awareness and sensitivity focused on action—action to preserve or action to change. We want our students to feel that they have the power to take this action, beginning in their communities and then expanding outward when the opportunity arises. This power to take action through modes of literacy is something our students can take with them out of our classrooms and into their futures. By having our students take, examine, and write about photographs depicting the communities in which they live, we can provide our students with such experiences.

When we look at the photographs of communities and community life taken by others and when we take and examine our own photographs of our surroundings and our communities, we learn to see. We learn to see not only what is there but also what is not there, or perhaps we become better at understanding what we see every day but don't often take notice of. We can begin to see the myriad social issues that surround us every day in our unique communities.

When we understand what we see, we may be able to respond to that understanding in ways that reinforce or support the positive and reassess or change the negative. Morrell (2002) writes about developing literacy through the use of popular culture. He defines an element of popular culture as "the everyday social experience of marginalized students as they confront, make sense of, and contend with social institutions such as schools, the mass media, corporations, and governments" (p. 73). We can expand upon this and say that photographs taken by students of the community in which they live and that surround the school where they go to learn represent the everyday life and social experience of the students.

Morrell (2002) notes that students who were writing about problems in their community were "motivated and empowered by the prospect of addressing a real problem in their community" and that they "learned the tools of research, read difficult texts, and produced their own text of high academic merit" (p. 77). Bomer and Bomer (2001), authors of *For a Better World: Reading and Writing for Social Action,* write that everyday concepts are "formed in activities outside of school," while school is a place where students formulate scientific concepts as they work with "explicit, organized support from a teacher" (p. 39). When you have students make visual records and writings based upon their observations in the communities where they live and go to school, you are helping them to make connections between their out-of-school and in-school knowledge and observations and to engage in practical applications of what they are learning.

If we want to empower our students to take action and effect positive change, we must help them experience this process while they are with us in school. For example, Fairbanks (2000) writes of a year-long inquiry project with students called "Write for Your Life." A sixth-grade teacher involved with the project helped her students identify what they called "kids' business" (p. 35). From this discussion of kids' business—or issues of concern to the young people in this particular community—students were able to generate a list of 45 topics they could investigate and write about. This experience helped students internalize a process whereby they could identify and later explore issues of concern in their community. Landay, Meehan, Newman, Wooton, and King (2001) write about a year-long project called "Postcards From America" in which high school students who had recently arrived in the United States photographed the people and places in their community. The students then wrote poetry and performed music, dance, and theater while their images, or "postcards," were projected on large screens. These students honed their skills of observation as they took a close look at the people and places in their community and then combined their pictorial discoveries with the arts to create a cultural event that focused on the diverse people, places, and positive elements in their community. We expand our views of literacy and the uses of literacy when we help students use observation, critical literacy, and authentic investigative writing experiences to act upon their world as they recognize what they can do to enhance their own lives and the lives of those in their communities.

In this chapter we will examine and reflect upon ways that we can use photographs to help our students develop understandings and write about their communities and the issues that concern them by having them participate in the following activities:

- Examine photographs that depict issues of social relevance
- Read a text about a social issue and respond by writing Found Poems to re-create the essence of the text
- Observe the community and write in their journals about problematic events or issues of concern
- Take photographs of their community to help them identify social issues
- Choose and write about an issue of social concern in the community

ACTIVITY 1

Looking at the World: Examining Photographs That Depict Issues of Social Relevance

You can begin to attend to issues of social relevance by first studying photographs that depict or refer to issues of social relevance. Hanson (2002) used photographs taken during the U.S. Great Depression by Walker Evans to help his sociology students "see the relationship between individual lives and the larger forces of politics and economics" (p. 236). Similarly, you can use photographs taken in communities from the past or present to reveal social issues that you want your students to explore. In this initial activity you might want to examine photographs that depict public transportation, libraries, well developed recreation areas, recycling plants, traffic jams, garbage in the streets and alleys, parks with broken and rusty playground equipment, graffiti, or other positive and negative elements of society that can lead to an exploration of specific social issues.

It helps to have the photographs in hand rather than ask students to search through magazines for pictures, which can be distracting. Therefore, first locate a photograph that depicts or refers to an issue of social relevance. Then, either make a transparency of the photograph or project it electronically so that you can engage your entire class in a close examination of this photo. At this time, you will, in fact, want to locate a number of photographs that depict social issues so that you have a collection on hand to use as a resource for the second part of this activity. When you collect the photographs, especially from magazines or newspapers, I recommend that you have them laminated to withstand wear.

As you search for photographs, try to choose images that lend themselves to reflection on social issues. For example, I have a photograph of a woman and a young girl, viewed from the back as they walk down a dirty, tile-floored hallway and another of a man holding the hand of a young boy and looking around him as they are surrounded by the crowds on an inner-city sidewalk. Both can help initiate thinking about social issues such as inner-city life and urban crowding, single parenthood, and so on. Look through old magazines and other sources to collect a number of photographs of people. Work with colleagues to identify photographs that lend themselves to reflection about social issues. You may want to examine the books listed in Table 7 to help generate ideas. You can also find photographs of social issues on the Internet. For example, the website content.lib.washington.edu/socialweb/index.html contains a database of historical images from Western and Pacific Northwest United States. Those related to women's issues, labor organizations, Japanese internment camps, and so on would provide images useful to this unit of study.

Table 7
Suggested Books for Reflection on Social Issues

Atkin, S.B. (2000). *Voices from the fields: Children of migrant farm workers tell their stories.* Boston: Little, Brown.
D'Amato, P. (2006). *Barrio: Photographs from Chicago's Pilsen and Little Village.* Chicago: University of Chicago Press.
Pinkney, S.L. (2006). *Read and rise.* New York: Scholastic.
Smith, C.R. (2003). *I am America.* New York: Scholastic.
Thomas, S.M. (1998). *Somewhere today: A book of peace.* Morton Grove, IL: Albert Whitman.
Wright, A. (2003). *Faces of hope: Children of a changing world.* Novato, CA: New World Library.

In my classroom, I often begin with a photograph taken by Walker Evans found in the book *Something Permanent* (Rylant, 1994). Evans traveled in America during the U.S. Great Depression taking photographs to document the cultural experiences, coping mechanisms, and survival tactics of ordinary people. Much later, author Cynthia Rylant chose Walker's photographs to be the subjects of poems she would write in this book. As my class examines the photograph, I read aloud the poem by Rylant that accompanies the photo I have selected. Her words help us "zoom" in on the elements of the photograph and understand it in new ways.

For example, in one of my classes, my students and I examined a transparency of a photograph of a smoke-stained brick fireplace surrounded by rough wood, once painted fresh white, now scratched and scarred. A wooden mantel above the fireplace is draped with an embroidered pillow cover. Carefully placed on the mantel is a chipped tin cup with a brush handle or spoon handle emerging from the cup. To the right of the cup is a wire rack with a tiny heart in the center. The rack holds some kind of paper. Beside that in the center of the mantel is a black travel clock with the hands at 10:00. Over to the right side of the mantel is a tiny cup next to a bottle of medicine. To the right of that is a small metal device, perhaps a pair of binoculars. Hanging above the mantel is a fireplace poker, a checked cotton bag with a string handle and a picture of a seated woman with a child sitting on her lap. The picture hangs crookedly from a tack.

Rylant's poem (1994, p. 26) accompanying this photo speaks to the reader about the woman who carefully placed these objects and who knows about beauty and wishes for summer when she can put flowers on the mantel. In my class we talked about how Rylant's words enhanced our reading of the photograph and focused our attention on the woman who cares for the room. One of my students, Martina, noted how the details of the photograph make the time period more "real" to her. Similarly, you will want to instruct students to take stock of all the elements in the photograph, reflect on the possible meaning of each object, and think about how the objects or people depicted relate to one another. What can students infer from these relationships?

After looking at a single photograph together as a whole class, provide students with the opportunity to examine and reflect on a photograph on their own. Begin by presenting students with a collection of photographs that depict people in places or situations that reflect social issues. Lay all the photographs face up on the floor or on a large table and ask students to walk around the exhibit and choose a photograph they want to examine and write about. After having each student choose a photograph, have students return to their desks and closely study the details in the photograph. It is helpful to provide a framework for observation of these details. Based upon questions posed by Flynn and McPhillips (2000, p. 135), ask students to study the photograph in detail, to reflect, and to write about "What do I notice?" "What do I wonder about?" and "What surprises me?" You may also want to provide them with some of the following additional questions and guiding phrases in order to further stimulate their thinking:

- What do I see? Search for details and list in an organized fashion everything you notice, beginning at the top and moving to the bottom, beginning at the bottom and moving to the top, beginning at the left and moving to the right, beginning at the right and moving to the left, beginning on the outside edges and moving to the inside, or beginning on the inside and moving to the outside edges.

- What might be happening here? Imagine the events that preceded the photograph or what might have happened after the photograph was taken. Move into the world of the picture.

- How might the person or persons in the photograph be feeling? As you look on the person and his or her surroundings, try to put yourself in this place and imagine what he or she might be feeling.

- Imagine what you would feel if you were in this situation and write about that.

- What do you wonder about the photograph? Have you noticed anything that seems out of place or that you cannot explain? Does looking at the photograph provoke questions for you?

- What surprises you? Is there something unexpected contained in or left out of the photograph?

REFLECTION POINT

Experiment with the questions provided for visual analysis and reflection. Is there any way you might want to adapt them to the needs and interests of your students?

For this part of the activity, one of my students, Kimberly, examined a photograph of a young woman walking down a dimly lit hallway with a dirty, mosaic-tile floor. The walls on either side of her are covered with grime and graffiti. We cannot see what is at the end of the hall. Two feet behind the young woman is a young girl wearing a cotton shirt that is too big for her and rubber sandals on her feet. Kimberly wrote the following:

- *What do I see?* Graffiti on the walls, dirty walls, black scum, dirty floor, enclosed hallway with little lighting and no windows. Project homes? Gang-related signs?

- *What might be happening here?* Two girls are walking down this hallway. The older girl seems to be in a hurry. Maybe she is afraid. This looks to be a kind of tough neighborhood. Does she belong here? Maybe something happened to them outside the building or someone said something to them that frightened her.

- *How might the person or persons in the photograph be feeling?* [I imagine that] I am eighteen years old and I have full responsibility for my little sister. I am on my way to get some food for us to eat. As I walk down this dark hall I'm thinking, "Why do I have to do this?" My sister lags behind me. I wish I could be more attentive to her, but it's not in my nature. My parents never were that way toward me. I wonder why my mom can't take care of my sister so I can be doing other things? I guess that's how my life is and always will be until I get out of here. I want to be in a different place.

- *How might I feel if I were in this photograph?* I feel irritated. So much is expected of me. I never have enough time to do the things I want to do. Everything in my life is "have to do." I feel like I missed my childhood.

- *What do I wonder about?* How do these people live? Why do they live here and how can they live here? Is it a safe place to stay? Is this a healthy environment?

- *What surprises me?* The child is walking behind the adult, carefree. The adult does not seem to acknowledge that the child is behind her.

When students have finished writing their observations about the photograph, it will enrich the experience if you invite them to share their images and what they have written with one another. Students can talk to a partner, or you may have a whole-class share. Sharing what they have noticed and what they have written helps alert them to different ways of seeing. As students view other images and think about them, their ideas about social issues in the community are expanding.

Reading Text Excerpts About Social Issues and Writing Found Poems

In order to extend your students' knowledge and understanding about social issues, you can follow up the preceding photo-centered activity with a text reading and writing activity. Select an informational book, article, or other text from the same time period you examined through the photos in Activity 1. Choose and mark a number of excerpts from the book that will give readers a complete preview of the text. Note that you will want to choose enough excerpts so that students may work in groups of two or three to write Found Poems, each group working with a different excerpt. Read the first text excerpt aloud to your class. As you read, work with your students to choose interesting or meaningful words and phrases from this text excerpt, and write these chosen words and phrases where the entire class can see them, such as on the board or on an overhead transparency.

Then, after the class has compiled a full list of significant words or phrases from the excerpt, work together to create a Found Poem based on the list. A Found Poem is created by choosing phrases or words from the original piece of text and shaping them into a poem "found" in the text excerpt. Once they see what a Found Poem is meant to look like and how it is created, instruct them to create their own. Divide students into groups and assign each group one of the remaining excerpts, instructing them to create a list of important words and phrases and then to turn that list into a Found Poem, as you have done together as a class.

For example, using my class's study of a Walker Evans photograph from the U.S. Great Depression, we next read excerpts from *Children of the Dust Bowl: The True Story of the School at Weedpatch Camp* (Stanley, 1992), an informational book about the same time period depicted in the photo we studied. This text describes the conditions that created the Dust Bowl and the journey from the Dust Bowl to migrant worker camps in California. The book chronicles the development of the Weedpatch Camp community and the school. This text was perfect for my purposes because it is illustrated with black-and-white photographs from this era and from Weedpatch Camp itself. I began by attempting to create a reading of excerpts that would give us a preview of the entire text, selecting a total of 11 excerpts. I read the first excerpt aloud to the class and then 10 small groups of students were assigned one of the other excerpts to read, discuss, and use as the basis for writing a Found Poem.

After I read the first excerpt out loud, we returned to the page and reread. I asked students to note words and phrases that stood out to them and that we might use in our poem. As the students called out the words and phrases, I wrote them on a transparency so that everyone in the class could see the following list:

> barren
> gambled with their lives
> bright and hot
> sizzling heat
> borrowed money to buy their land
> borrowed again against their land
> one thousand families a week...were losing their farms to the banks (Stanley, 1992, p. 3)

Using this list as a base, we added words and phrases to create the following Found Poem:

> Hard, barren depression—
> Heartache.

Impossible situation...
They gambled with their lives.
Sky bright and hot—
Sizzling heat.
Crops shriveled up.
No irrigation canals and reservoirs.
Lives shriveled up.
A thousand families a week went to the bank,
Borrowed money for land...
Borrowed against the land...
Borrowed time...
Bargained and lost.

We read our Found Poem out loud in a choral reading and then the students joined their groups to read the other excerpts from the text and create their own Found Poems. As they worked, I moved behind them, listening to their voices and reading over their shoulders. When they finished, I invited them to read around the circle. We read our Found Poems in the order of the pages excerpted from the text. The following is the Found Poem written by Dana, Jorge, and Luz based on an excerpt from the text:

The Panhandle is flat,
so I could see dust storms coming.
The dust was red
and the air looked like a
wave of blood
racing to envelop and
suffocate us all.
The dust clouds were so dangerous
they could scare the animals away.
That's when we knew that
we too,
had to go away.
Dust clouds came and went,
day after day.
None ever brought rain.

As we created and shared our Found Poems, we formed ideas about a variety of different genres, the time period, and the multiple voices and points of view of the people who lived at this time. In addition, reading an excerpt in order to discuss it and create a Found Poem alerted us to important words, phrases, and ideas. As we reshaped or reformulated the text in order to create a poem, we developed further understanding and ownership of the text. You might also use this method to provide students with a general overview of a historical era. For example, to introduce students to the decade from 1930 to 1940, I chose excerpts from the books listed in Table 8.

Table 8
Texts Used to Introduce Students to Social Issues of the 1940s

Ehrenburg, I., & Simonov, K. (1985). *In one newspaper: A chronicle of unforgettable years* (A. Kagan, Trans.). New York: Sphinx Press.

Fujita, F. (1955). *Foo: A Japanese–American prisoner of the rising sun*. Denton: University of North Texas Press.

Hall, R. (1957). *You're stepping on my cloak and dagger*. New York: W.W. Norton.

Pershing, J.J. (1931). *My experiences in the World War*. New York: Frederick A. Stokes.

Pope, D. (1958). *73 north: The defeat of Hitler's navy*. Philadelphia: J.B. Lippincott.

Reynolds, Q. (1944). *The curtain rises*. New York: Random House.

Shukert, E.B., & Scibetta, B.S. (1988). *War brides of World War II*. Novato, CA: Presidio Press.

Shull, M.S., & Wilt, D.E. (1996). *Hollywood war films, 1937–1945: An exhaustive filmography of American feature-length motion pictures relating to World War II*. Jefferson, NC: McFarland & Company.

Terkel, S. (1984). *"The good war": An oral history of World War II*. New York: Pantheon Books.

Tregaskis, R. (1943). *Guadalcanal diary*. New York: Random House.

REFLECTION POINT

This activity could be used to help stimulate your students' background knowledge for a novel or short story they will be reading or to support students' reading of a social studies textbook. Can you think of other ways you could use this strategy?

ACTIVITY **3**

"Reading" the Community and Writing Journal Entries About Issues That Concern Us

Now that students have had the opportunity to write about social issues in the world, they will make the experience more personal by "reading" their own communities in order to identify and write about relevant social issues that hit closer to home. When we ask our students to "read" the community we are asking them to heighten their sense of awareness and their skills of observation as they move about in the community. Heightened awareness and skills of observation as well as the habit of recording what we observe should be of benefit to writers in general. In particular, this will be of benefit to writers who will be writing to inform, persuade, or call to action. These writers will strengthen their work through the sense of immediacy in their work and the vivid details of the sights, sounds, and smells they bring from their writer's journals to their final pieces.

When students are in the habit of writing in notebooks or journals, it is less difficult to ask them to transition and include their observations of social issues. Because your students have been using a writer's journal throughout the year and with the activities described throughout this book, your students have their journals with them at all times, and they are already open to and aware of the world around them. Still, it may not be enough to simply invite your students to begin recording their observations of problematic events or social issues of concern. Therefore, you may need to demonstrate the process for your students with an example or two from your own journal. You may want to share some general entries first, but it's most important for you to share an entry or two about a social issue or problem that you have observed.

Bomer and Bomer (2001) note that "it's hard for teachers to help students learn to write in a particular way...unless we do some of the same sort of writing ourselves," and that teachers can demonstrate writing of two kinds: "after the fact and in the midst" (p. 116). "After the fact" entries can be shared as a read-aloud or printed onto a transparency. Key questions to help students begin writing about social issues of concern might be "Is this right?" "Is this fair?" and/or "Is there something I/we could do about this?" When you demonstrate this for your students with your own journal, you will want to reflect on one or more of these questions. For example, I shared the following entry from my journal about something I had encountered that I thought would interest my students.

Is this right? My students and I sit together as a class at lunch. It is a school rule that students are not permitted to move to other tables to sit with the students in other classes. When they finish eating they cannot get up and move around; they have to stay seated until the dismissal bell rings and then we all walk back to class together.

In the last few months, the weather has been great. We decided to take our lunches out to the enclosed patio and eat and talk. It was really nice for my students because it is quieter out there and they could enjoy visiting more. When they finished eating they could walk around a bit. Some of them began to bring board games they could play with their friends. It's only natural that other students, when they saw what we were doing, would want to do the same. It wasn't long before it got fairly crowded out on the patio. Sometimes three or four class groups were out there at one time.

Soon after this occurred, we received a note from the principal telling us that we would no longer be allowed to eat on the patio. This may be fair—if this many people are in such a small space, someone could get hurt. Teachers can't watch out for this many people in a constricted space. What can I do about it? I am thinking that I will make a proposal to the principal that we enjoy the patio on a rotating basis. I can bring my class one day, Ms. Browning can bring hers out on another, and so on. This plan is a nice compromise—it allows my students a bit of freedom and I can still watch out for them.

After you share your entry with your students, talk about what you've done in the journal entry. For example, in my class, we discussed that in my entry I have done the following:

- Observed something that is happening
- Noted what others think or feel about the event or issue
- Thought about what I could do or what others could do to alleviate the situation
- Reflected on my feelings about the ramifications or potential effects of the issue

Although these guidelines are not specific requirements for an entry, they are helpful for how students might begin writing.

Another way to demonstrate the process for students is to write "in the midst" (Bomer & Bomer, 2001, p. 116) entries. "In the midst" entries could be written by teachers and students together at the point where an observation is made. I would imagine that there are a number of problematic or social issues occurring in and around your classrooms each day. I remember an issue that occurred in another school where I taught seventh graders who were allowed to choose where they sat at lunch time. Stephano, one of my seventh-grade students, was concerned about the way that some students were ostracized during the lunch period and had to sit by themselves at a table away from the others. Stephano wrote about this in his journal and shared what he had written with his classmates before we left for lunch one day. At his urging, a group of students decided to move to this table and attempt to "get to know" the outsiders. Stephano could have written his ideas on a transparency and incorporated the ideas of his fellow students to demonstrate how we might write about a problem or social issue in our community.

Several days later, after you have shared more examples from your own journal and your students have had opportunities to record their own observations of the community in their own writer's journals, your students may be ready to share. These entries that students have written both inside and outside of the classroom, when shared aloud in class or with partners, form the basis for students' thinking and further writing about social issues of relevance to them. For example, a sixth grader might write and share an entry like the following:

> This is my first year to have a yearbook in school. My parents couldn't really afford to buy me one, but they knew it was important to me so they helped me "earn" the money by

doing things around the house. They even let me help out some of the neighbors. The point is, I worked hard to buy my yearbook and it means a lot to me. Is this right?

When we got our yearbooks, everyone wanted their friends to write something in the blank pages at the back. The teachers told us that we could spend the first few minutes in class passing our yearbooks around for people to sign. The problem is some kids like me don't really know a lot of people they could ask to sign. I just moved here recently and I feel I don't have a lot of friends yet. It only took me a few minutes to get the friends I do have to sign my book. Now, I am sitting in class trying to look like I have something else important to do while the other kids are signing books.

I can see how other kids that do know a lot of people would want to get their books signed. What could I do to help? Maybe we could have one day when the kids who wanted to get their yearbooks signed by their friends could stay after school. Well, that wouldn't work because we all ride the bus. Maybe we could do something in the morning when we are all waiting in the cafeteria for the bell to ring. At least with that big of a crowd, those of us who don't know many people wouldn't stand out so much.

After students have had the opportunity to share their thoughts with the class, work with your students to brainstorm and create a class list of social issues of interest. Some topics you might consider include the following:

Animal shelters

Littering

Recycling

Homelessness

Cliques in schools

Racism

Teen pregnancy

Failing

Dealing with homework

Neighborhood playgrounds and/or parks

After-school activities

Being home alone

Watching over younger brothers and sisters

REFLECTION POINT

What are some of the issues of concern in your community? What do you notice as you travel to and from school? What do you notice when you are in school? Could any of these be topics for you to write about?

Can you think of other ways to help your students identify and begin thinking about social issues?

ACTIVITY 4

Taking Pictures in Our Own Communities and Reading Them

Throughout this book, photographs have been used as a tool to help us see further and deeper into the relationships between people, places, and objects—now you will use photographs to help students see further and deeper into the social issues students have identified as relevant to their communities. This activity will also help students identify the social issues they will write about for the final activity in this chapter. However, before you have students proceed into their communities with cameras in hand, it would be helpful to share some of your own photographs of the community with students. Sharing your own photos from the community will give students a level of comfort as they take their own photos.

Try taking some photographs of the area around the school where you teach. Look for elements or scenes that suggest social issues. Choose several of your photographs and reproduce them in a way that you can share with your students. You may make transparencies of your pictures or you may be able to project them electronically. Describe your process for taking pictures to help you see your community in new ways. Take your students for a "walk" through the community using your photographs as visual stimulus for discussion of social issues. You will want to caution your students to take photographs from a place of safety and to respect the privacy of others. Depending upon your students and the community in which they live, you may want to develop specific guidelines for your students.

For example, I might share with my students the photo Figure 18, a photograph I took while walking down a neighborhood street in the community near my school. As I project the photograph where all can see, I think aloud. The house is painted a pretty light aqua. Several of the boards are rotting at the edges and one has been replaced but not painted. The white painted window frame is also rotting in the lower left-hand corner. There is a rusting chain-link fence at the edge of the yard near the sidewalk. There are metal dogs on top of the gate and a metal horse head on the fence post. A sign on the gate warns us to "Beware of the Dog." Placed on the windowsill, so we can see it as we walk by, is an acrylic painting of a seaside cottage. I am in Galveston, Texas, USA, a seaside community. The sea air can be fairly corrosive, and I wonder if the owner of this house has trouble keeping up with all the repairs and painting of the house. Later, I see him leaning on the fence, talking to a neighbor. I think he must appreciate beautiful things, and because

Figure 18
Photo of a House in the Community

he wants to share his love of beauty with us, he has put his painting in the window, facing out where all can see it.

Another photo I took in Galveston is depicted in Figure 19. I took this photo of a diner while driving down one of the downtown streets. Outside, an electric scooter with a straw basket and an American flag attached is parked at an angle near the door. I wonder if it is safe to leave the scooter outside. I wonder if the building is handicap accessible. I wonder if the owner of the scooter left it here on the sidewalk because there is no room to maneuver around the tables and chairs inside. I think about the challenges for individuals who are less mobile.

After you have modeled photographing scenes from the community, instruct students to take their own photographs in their communities or in the community where the school is located with digital or disposable cameras. Instruct students to focus on two to three sites and then take several photographs of each site, presenting it from different angles. Once students have had the opportunity to take their photographs, have them bring in their photographs printed on photographic paper or grouped on printer paper and then take turns sharing

Figure 19
Photo Taken Outside of a Diner in the Community

with the class. Each photographer should spread his or her photographs out on the table in the center of the room, and the class can stand in a circle around the table, looking and listening. Students should each talk about their process and "read" what social issues they see in the photographs as they talk.

As they talk about their photographs students will recognize the issue of greatest concern to them. As their peers listen to what they say, they should ask refining questions and offer suggestions to the presenter. This process allows students to refine their thinking as they read the photograph and then decide what they will focus on when they write about the photographs and the related issue of social concern. This is an important experience to give to our students. Oftentimes they rely upon us to help them generate and formulate ideas. With this exercise students share the photographs of events or scenes that strike them as being meaningful and that may represent potential issues of social relevance. As students talk and question one another, they begin to see how they can support one another and, eventually, how they can become thinking and writing resources for themselves.

Figure 20
Juan's Photo of Graffiti

For example, in one of my classes, Juan talked about his photographs of the broken-down fences in his neighborhood and about the photographs of the neighborhood that depict graffiti, wondering, "Why do young people join gangs?" (see Figure 20). In the taking of the photographs and in the talk about the photographs, Juan has identified what he will write about. It is clear that the issues of graffiti and young people in gangs concern him.

Another student, Sana, shared photographs of a street corner and the back of a man who appears to have been living on the street for some time. Sana told us about Red, a homeless man she has watched and given food to for a number of years. She says,

> I asked Red about some of the hardships he must face from living on the streets. He said that cold, rainy nights like the weather has been these last few days are hard on him because of his arthritis. I asked him where he slept to get out of the rain. Red pointed to this shopping center [Sana points to the photograph] across the street that has a large overhanging roof. He also pointed out that his shopping cart over here [Sana shows photograph] up against one of the buildings was out of the rain. He said he prefers the heat to cold weather any day of the week.

After sharing these photos and reflections, Sana decided to interview and write about Red, and during her interview with Red, Sana gained an insider's perspective on the issues confronting the homeless.

REFLECTION POINT

Can you think of other ways to facilitate a sharing and decision-making discussion in your classroom? Would your students listen as a whole class as I have suggested, or would it be more productive for them to work in small groups or with a partner? What might your role be during these discussions?

ACTIVITY 5

Choosing and Writing About a Social Issue in the Community

As students engaged in the preceding activities in this chapter, they constructed the knowledge set they will now need for the final activity: writing about a single issue of social relevance. Through the previous discussions in Activity 4, students were able to refine their ideas in presentation and discussion, and this helps them narrow down a single issue on which to focus for the writing activity and to select a specific photograph or photographs to use as the inspiration for the writing. However, while the initial decisions may be made as students talk about their photographs with the class group, more discussion in needed. Therefore, have your students meet with you in individual conferences or with peers in response groups so that they can make determinations about the purpose and focus for the pieces they will write for the final writing activity.

Students should write two pieces in two different genres. The first piece should be one in which students gather information about the issue. They may conduct an in-depth observation at the site they have photographed, or they may write a detailed description of the site and its relationship to the surrounding community or environment. Alternatively, students could write an informational piece in which they gather data about the issue or site from a number of sources and report what they have learned. The second piece should move deeper into the issue. The writer may interview someone who might provide additional knowledge or assistance related to the issue, or the writer may compose a piece that is a proposal or a call to action. This might be an article for a community newsletter or a letter to a person who might approve or take action related to the issue.

In order to provide a view of the social issues that may be identified and written about by your students, the following are some examples from the work of my own students. One student, Violet, wrote about neighborhood decay and rebirth. For this project, she walked through her neighborhood, one of the oldest in this city. She described what she was seeing as she walked and provided her readers with some historical background about the neighborhood, as illustrated in the following text (see Figures 21 and 22 for the photos that accompanied her project):

If one were to look at these pictures they might think they were taken somewhere in the wilderness or out in the country. This is just one small portion of a community called Fifth

Figure 21
Photo of Violet's House

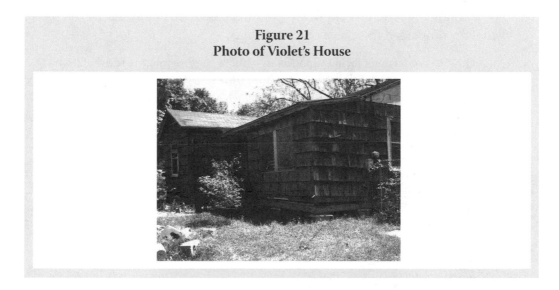

Figure 22
Photo of Vinegar Plant Near Violet's House

Ward. This is where I live. It has been my home for all of my life. This house might not be the biggest or prettiest but it has kept my family and me safe. The history of this place, the people who called and still call this place home, and the place itself is fading away. But across the tracks and past the simple rows of houses is a sign of a slow rebirth of the community.

...the vinegar plant has been a nuisance over the years. There have been times when the air literally smells like vinegar. One year the factory had to scare off sparrows with a mechanical bird that screeched every ten minutes...the plant is also a large reason why the field next to it is contaminated. On this fence are posters some protesters have placed there about the contaminated field.

The second piece to Violet's project was an interview with her father about his feelings about the community and the "changing times in the Fifth Ward." The following is an excerpt from that interview (see Figure 23 for the photo that accompanied this piece of the writing):

Q: What do you think about the possibility of more people coming here to build who have the money like the people across the railroad tracks?

A: The possibility of that happening is quite high because they've already begun to build townhouses on Clinton Street. Fifth Ward is attracting a lot of people because of the close proximity to the downtown area. The first place they might build in our area would be the vinegar plant. They have already had reports out on cleaning up the field.

Q: You mentioned the vinegar plant.... I have felt it has been somewhat of a nuisance to our community. What are your feelings toward the plant?

A: Well, yeah, it has been a nuisance. You might remember when the explosion happened where a man was thrown from one of the towers into the gulley. That was real unfortunate. I don't really have any ill feelings toward the plant, but I also would not mind seeing it go if it comes to that....

Figure 23
Violet's Photo to Accompany Interview

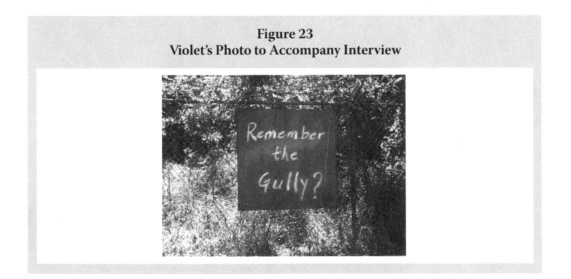

When students engage in learning experiences such as this, it is important to reflect upon their processes and the outcome. You may want to invite your students to complete a reflective paragraph following their experience in investigating and writing about a social issue of concern from their community. For example, one of my students, Lana, reflected on the process as a whole, writing the following:

> Writing about a social issue is very sensitive, especially when the issue is something that you can relate to. However, writing about the social issue allows you the opportunity to discover feelings and facts that you never knew. There are so many things that you find out when you take the time to observe and to read, and there are even more things that become evident when you write....

Sana wrote the following about having a choice:

> I really enjoyed the social issue genre pieces we have been working on. I like the fact that it was something that I was able to choose. I chose the issue of homelessness for my social issue. It wasn't a difficult decision for me because this is something that is close to my heart. It is something that I encounter on a daily basis living in this city. I also have a friend who was homeless for a while and this is one of my big fears....

Juan wrote about where we go from here:

> I enjoyed writing about a social issue. It made me think about if there was one thing that I wanted to change, what would it be?

REFLECTION POINT

Think about your expectations for your students. How many pieces do you want them to write? How would you like them to present their work? Do you have a school website where they could possibly publish their work? Can you work with the school media specialist to set up an exhibit of their photographs and writings? Would you invite community members to view an exhibit?

Conclusion

When we work with our students to examine photographs that depict issues of social relevance, to look for visual details, and to analyze photographs through reflection and writing based upon guiding questions, we begin the process of confronting social issues through images. When we read texts about social issues and create Found Poems from the texts and when we write in our journals about issues or events that concern us, we begin to confront social issues through words. When we take photographs and talk about them with others to help us formulate ideas about what issues we will focus upon, we are using images to help us name and think about how we will confront a particular social issue. However, when we use these photographs as starting points and then write about issues of social concern, we are beginning to confront social issues through action.

It is likely that many of our students will choose to take action after they have written about issues of social concern. When creating the final project in which she wrote about a social issue of relevance to the community, one of my students, Shameeka, wrote about the poor conditions of her neighborhood playground. Her first piece was an observation in which she compared and contrasted the playground in her neighborhood with one in a more affluent neighborhood. Following this, Shameeka asked fourth and fifth graders in her neighborhood if they would participate in a group interview about the playground. During the interview process, she and the others generated a number of ideas about how they could make this place a site they would want to go to relax and enjoy themselves. Shameeka decided to go to her church and ask if there was a way that a project to clean up the playground could be funded by the members. The church members agreed that Shameeka could publicize her background research and her ideas in the church newsletter. There is a possibility that social action will occur as a result of Shameeka's work in identifying and writing about an issue of social concern.

Similarly, I believe that we can help many of our students identify pathways and possibilities for taking action in their communities. When students cannot take direct action, they may be able to transform what they have written into letters that can be sent to community leaders and/or neighborhood action groups. When we do such things, we are uniting our communities and taking actions that help us develop partnerships with all of the stakeholders in our students' education.

REFERENCES

Bomer, R., & Bomer, K. (2001). *For a better world: Reading and writing for social action.* Portsmouth, NH: Heinemann.

Fairbanks, C.F. (2000). Fostering adolescents' literacy engagements: "Kid's business" and critical inquiry. *Reading Research and Instruction, 40,* 35–50.

Flynn, N., & McPhillips, S. (2000). *A note slipped under the door: Teaching from poems we love.* Portland, ME: Stenhouse.

Hanson, C.M. (2002). A stop sign at the intersection of history and biography: Illustrating Mills's imagination with Depression-era photographs. *Teaching Sociology, 30,* 235–242.

Landay, E., Meehan, M.B., Newman, A.L., Wooton, K., & King, D.W. (2001). "Postcards from America": Linking classroom and community in an ESL class. *English Journal, 90*(5), 66–74.

Morrell, E. (2002). Toward a critical pedagogy of popular culture: Literacy development among urban youth. *Journal of Adolescent & Adult Literacy*, *46*, 72–77.

LITERATURE CITED

Rylant, C. (1994). *Something permanent.* New York: Harcourt Brace.
Stanley, J. (1992). *Children of the Dust Bowl: The true story of the school at Weedpatch Camp.* New York: Crown.

CHAPTER 5

Envisioning People, Places, and Events: Reading Photographs to Write Narratives

HER NAME IS GRACE. She is the only child of Lucille and Melvin. She sits outside in the front yard of the house they rent in Oil City, Pennsylvania, USA. Her

daddy works for Oilwell Supply Company. Her mama stays at home and takes care of both of them. Grace entertains herself with imaginary friends. Right now she is playing house. She and her doll friends Emmaline and Louellen are seated at a doll-size table in the front yard. Grace has set out teacups and plates for each of them. Emmaline, the baby, is too young to drink from a cup, but Louellen, the same age as Grace, will do so. Grace, her feet primly aligned, her

left hand resting in her lap, is sipping "tea" while looking at her mother, who is taking the picture. Soon, her mother will join her at the table. She will pull the wrought-iron chair from behind the fir tree shading the porch and sit with Grace. They will visit, softly clicking their teacups as they set them in the saucers after each sip, talking about the weather, Grace's lovely hair bow, the roast Lucille will make for dinner. They'll thread together a life that is at once real and imaginary.

As I look at this photograph of my mother as a young girl, I try to put myself inside the picture. I look at what is there and imagine what might be happening in this moment. As I think further, I imagine what might be happening in the moments surrounding this moment and that is when the story, or the narrative, begins to form in my mind.

In our classrooms we can use single photographs or a series of photographs to help us generate narratives. When student writers have the opportunity to work from visual images, they may include greater levels of detail in their writing. They may also write about topics or characters they might not have dreamed of when working solely from the images in their minds. Westcott (1997) writes that "photographs can become subject matter for talking and writing" (p. 53). He notes that "photographs that suggest stories can stimulate story telling by students and, more importantly, give them insights into how important suggestion (as opposed to detailed exposition) can be in writing narrative" (p. 53). Westcott suggests that students might be encouraged to take their own photographs. He describes an activity in which groups of students take one or two photographs and then work together to refine and develop the positioning and lighting in the photograph. Through this process, students "revise" a photograph to make it more effective. This revision process can be compared to the process in which writers engage.

Middle school and high school students may be less aware than elementary school students of the visual aspects of literacy. With the exception of their textbooks, the materials they read in school may have few, if any, illustrations or photographs. Without opportunities to consider, "read," and talk about visual images, readers learn to focus more on text and less, if at all, on visual images. Garrett-Petts (2000) relates an experience of his colleague Karen Day, who teaches language arts in a university:

> One afternoon she held up a copy of Pat Hutchins's *Rosie's Walk*, a book with illustrations and text arranged separately on alternate pages, and asked the class what they noticed. "Every other page is blank," suggested one of her students, apparently confident that the words, not the images were of principal interest. (p. 39)

Garrett-Petts (2000) explains that a "muted" assumption held by many readers, publishers, and educators is that "visual elements in a text may be safely ignored, marginalized, or simply edited out" (p. 39). Nodelman (1991) urges us to understand that readers of all ages will become more competent and adept at meaning making if they can recognize and manipulate what he calls the three potential stories of picture books: the one in the pictures, the one in the words, and the one that results as the pictures and words are integrated or combined. The third story in which text and image are combined provides the reader with a new challenge and produces a more complex response (Garrett-Petts, 2000). It is that third story that we are focused upon in this chapter. As we think about creating narratives based upon images, we are focused upon what happens when an image provokes or causes a story to form—what happens when an image and text are integrated by the writer rather than the reader.

As we help our students become more visually literate, we can also help them to become aware of how images and texts may seek to position readers or control what and how they respond and react to images and texts.

Through the daily literacy experiences in which we engage with our students, we can help them become more visually and critically literate. Alvermann and Hagood (2000) urge us to consider that "critical media literacy is a natural and necessary component of day-to-day literacy instruction, not a unit of instruction to be taught over two weeks" (p. 201). Becoming visually and critically literate is closely related to narrative writing, in that writers of stories need to heighten their awareness of the ways that words and images convey meaning. Powerful narratives emerge when writers attend to what is there and what is not there and when they know and understand that the absence or inclusion of a thing or an idea creates meaning.

In this chapter we will examine and reflect upon ways that we can use photographs to help our students critically read images and use images as the impetus for writing narratives as we engage them in the following activities:

- Critically read images
- Analyze visual images and text in magazine advertisements for denotations (what we literally see) and connotations (implications or implied meaning of what we see)
- Identify the elements of a narrative through picture books and wordless texts
- Write a narrative with a partner
- Write a two-voice narrative based upon an encounter or situation and a narrative based upon an art reproduction or other book illustration individually
- Write a narrative based upon personal photographs

ACTIVITY 1

Zooming In on an Image: Critical Readings of Images

Alvermann, Moon, and Hagood (1999) write that "the meaning of a written message, a visual image, or a sound bite rests not in the thing itself but instead in us, the audience—the reader, the viewer, the listener" (p. 129). As you read, look, and listen, you might call upon your prior knowledge about the thing or the concept. You might think about how your own personal experiences relate to the message.

How can you best illustrate for your students that prior knowledge, personal experiences, and being aware of how we develop our understandings all may influence how we interpret and respond to new visual messages? I like to begin with a "reading" of the picture texts *Re-Zoom* and *Zoom* by Istvan Banyai (1995a, 1995b). Both of these books challenge us by presenting an image and then altering our perception of the image. For example, in *Zoom*, we look first at a drawing of a rooster. The next picture shows us a view that is farther away from the rooster. Here we can see a young girl and boy standing on a wooden stool, looking at the rooster from a cottage window. We move farther back to see a white stucco farmhouse, then farther still to see a group of farmhouses, then farther still to see a girl reaching out to touch the "farmhouses," which are on a table in a toy shop. We move farther still to see that this is actually an image of a toy shop on the cover of a magazine held by a boy who is sleeping in a chair on the deck of a cruise ship. As we continue to read the images, we move farther and farther away from the initial image of the rooster until finally we leave the earth behind and see it only as a small white dot in the center of a black page. As we look at the images, we realize that each thing we see is in reality not what we think but a part of an even larger world.

As you "read" the wordless text with your students, have students talk about their discoveries of the actuality of the images and how you "know" what you know. Talk about how the illustrator fools the reader by playing on what might be the most obvious interpretation of each image and then surprises you by showing you something you did not expect to see. This experience not only provides an opportunity for you to talk to your students about how you might read images but also allows you to discuss how your thoughts can be manipulated by images and our understanding or response to them. Your students will likely be fascinated by these books and want to look at them on their own after you view them as a whole class. Perhaps you may know of other texts or images that you could also use to help your students comprehend the way that our prior knowledge, personal experiences, and awareness of how we develop understandings impact how we interpret and respond to new visual messages.

On their own, several of my students, inspired by our readings of these texts, created wordless texts, building a story from images. In order to build upon the observation activity, you may want to ask your students to do the same. Students may digitize photographs or use digital photographs in a PowerPoint presentation of a "wordless text." Others may prefer to draw their own wordless stories on printer paper folded and stapled in the center to form a pamphlet or "comic book" format. For example, one of my students, Darry, created a PowerPoint presentation of a "book" he wrote about his 3-year-old nephew Denny. The text is illustrated with photographic images he has borrowed from the Internet. In his project, Darry reversed the process in *Zoom* and *Re-Zoom*. Rather than starting with the close-up and moving farther away and out into the universe, Darry begins with the Milky Way and takes us to Earth; to the North American continent; to the United States; to Washington, DC; to a neighborhood; to a house; and finally into Denny's crib as we view a picture of Denny, who is wearing a onesie and a knitted cap and is smiling up at us. Darry continues the story of Denny, showing us Denny's parents, his kitten, his aunt and uncle, and some of the things he likes to do for fun. Darry closes with the words, "The story of Denny will be continued...." Darry tells us he plans to add to the story and give it to Denny one day when "he's old enough to appreciate it."

REFLECTION POINT

My student Darry used his experience with *Zoom* and *Re-Zoom* to help him write a biography of his nephew. Are there other types of stories that could be written? Could you and your students search for images on the Internet or in magazines and create a book similar to this?

ACTIVITY **2**

Examining Magazine Advertisements for Denotations and Connotations

By weaving daily experiences in visual and critical literacy into our curriculum, you can help your students become more aware of the messages conveyed with words and images. This awareness will tie directly into narrative writing when writers use it to help them make decisions about what to include and leave out of their stories. One way you can provide your students with experience in viewing images and texts and beginning to critically read images and texts is by studying magazine advertisements in a structured way. Therefore, in this activity, you will invite your students to examine a magazine advertisement and identify and talk about the denotations and connotations of the image and text (if text is included).

Denotations are based upon what we literally see when we look at an image. To denote means to signify, to mean, or to be the symbol of. For example, if I look at the photograph in Figure 24 of a man holding the hand of a child as they walk, I see the man and the child and how they are positioned. I might denote from this image the idea of fatherhood and that of love or safety. To me, a man holding the hand of a child symbolizes, signifies, or means these things. *Connotations* are based upon the implications of the things we see *or* the words we read. A connotation is a secondary or implied meaning. For

Figure 24
Photo of Unidentified Man Holding the Hand of a Child

From Library of Congress Prints and Photographs Online Catalog. Image of a Chinese child with an adult on step outside of building, Chinatown, New York City. Part of the George Grantham Bain Collection. Retrieved October 26, 2007, from hdl.loc.gov/loc.pnp/cph.3c20168

example, looking at the same photograph, I might connote or understand an implied meaning that fathers should love and protect their children.

Barrett (2003) writes that "denotations and connotations are at play in all of visual and verbal communication, and their consequences can be much more serious than designers' attempts at influencing our choices of which fashions to desire and acquire" (p. 6). He cites the work of Barthes (1977), who investigated how cultural items signify meaning. Barthes studied magazine advertisements for their linguistic message, denoted image, and connoted image. When we work with our students we can combine the linguistic message or written text with the connoted image. This simplifies the process when we examine magazine advertisements because the linguistic message most often aids the viewer in arriving at or understanding the connotations of the piece. When Hamilton (2000) and her students work with photographs, she has her students create a two-column chart with "Elements visible within literacy events (These may be captured in photographs)" on the left and

"Non-visible constituents of literacy practices (These may only be inferred from photographs)" on the right (p. 17).

Following an example that defines denotation and connotation and how these can be used to understand a photo's message, work as a whole class to analyze a magazine advertisement. It may be helpful to begin with an image *without* words and then move to an image *with* words, as I often do in my classrooms. Then, engage the class in a discussion of the denotations and connotations they observe in this advertisement. Through your questioning and discussion, you can help your students verbalize their understandings.

For example, in one of my classes, I began with an advertisement for women's clothing that does not include text. I projected this image onto a screen where all could see it at once. The room grew silent for a moment as we looked at this perfectly tanned, curvaceous woman dressed in fringed buckskin pants; a tight, turquoise jersey shirt; straw cowboy hat; and high-heeled boots. One student, Susan, remarked, "I never look like that when *I* go to the rodeo." I asked the class, "Where is this woman?" trying to get them to look beyond the person to her surroundings. "She's just on a flat surface," commented Jodi. "Like a paper background for the photograph," someone added. "Look closer, what else do you see?" Suddenly there was an explosion of laughter and "Oh my!" from the students. Daniella noted something and pointed it out to those who sit near her. The woman in the advertisement is strapped to the background with thin elastic bands. "Like Barbie!" announced Shameeka. "And that's not all," intoned Maria. "Look at the other things in the photograph—her accessories, the rope, and the other stuff—they're held down by the bands as well." "What are they tryin' to say here?" demanded Jodi. As we thought about it, the ideas flew and the noise in the room accelerated. "Women are like Barbie dolls—they come with accessories, and you can keep them in the box or dress them up and take them out." We talked about the Italian designer whose product is advertised with this image. Do the connotations we determine from our critical analysis of the advertisement sell the product to us? Do we want to be like dolls or toys? We decided that, for us, the advertisement has failed.

Next, we examined an image of a young girl about 8 years old with her hair in pigtails. She is standing in what looks to be her bedroom, which is painted lavender. There is a lavender chair with brightly colored cushions behind her. Above the chair a montage of photographs, cards, and documents is arranged on the wall, not on a bulletin board. She stands beside an iron bed that is painted white. Beside the bed is a window. Outside the window it is a sunny day. With two hands holding a large piece of tissue up to her nose, the little girl appears to be blowing her nose. As we looked at the image and noted the contents, the denotation that came to us is that the little girl is sick or has a sinus condition. When we included our reading of the accompanying text, however, our thoughts were modified. The text reads, "Ruthless killer." Surely this is not a commentary or description to be associated with the little girl. "Well, is there anything else in the photograph that could be linked with the words *ruthless killer*?" I asked. "The tissue, the tissue!" exclaimed Daniella. Something interesting occurred when she said this. We realized that we were attracted to the advertisement because we wanted to understand why anyone would refer to a cute little girl as a "ruthless killer." Our attraction led us to study the image further and to read the small print. As we did so, we came to understand that the "ruthless killer" is the antiviral tissue that "traps and kills" germs. It is not only the words but also the positioning of the objects in the image that helped us come to this conclusion. In this image the tissue and the hands of the little girl are the objects that are closest to the viewer.

As you examine the magazine advertisements as a class, you may want to create a list of the connotations and denotations the students observe. Then, invite your students to choose a magazine advertisement and to work in small groups to identify the denotations and connotations. You might also have students examine historical advertisements from the Ad Access Project funded by the Duke Endowment "Library 2000" Fund. Advertisements from 1911 through 1955 are included at the website scriptorium.lib.duke.edu/adaccess. When all of the groups have had an opportunity to analyze a piece, invite them to show their magazine advertisement and share their thoughts with their peers. Viewers may add to the interpretation with thoughts of their own.

REFLECTION POINT

Rather than focus on advertisements for household products or those directed to adults, what do you think would be the impact of analyzing advertisements for products that are being sold to your students?

ACTIVITY 3

Identifying Elements in a Narrative

Your students are most likely natural storytellers. Even so, it can be helpful for you to think about the elements contained in a narrative before you begin an intense focus on this genre. One way you can do this is to read aloud and analyze a picture book. Another way is for students to write stories to go along with wordless texts. After this, students will be ready to work alone or with a partner to create a story "live" as you prompt them with general questions or suggestions.

Identifying Elements in a Narrative Using Picture Books

To help students identify the elements of a narrative in a picture book, choose and read aloud as a class a picture book that has a clearly identified setting, characters, events, problem or conflict, and solution or resolution. For example, I like to use a picture book written by Kathi Appelt (2002) titled *Bubba and Beau, Best Friends*. This picture book is divided up into "chapters," and in the text you'll learn about a family who lives in Lubbock, Texas, USA. Bubba is the son of Big Bubba and Mama Pearl. Beau, a hound puppy, is the son of Maurice and Evelyn. Bubba and Beau are best friends: "they both went around on all fours, they were both keen on chewing, neither one was house-trained. And they could howl to beat the band. They also had a mutual affection for mud and a mutual disdain for soap." Both Bubba and Beau loved a little pink blankie. Bubba loved the blankie because it smelled like Beau, and Beau loved it because it smelled like Bubba. Disaster occurs when Mama Pearl decides to wash the blankie and it then smells like soap. Bubba and Beau are heartbroken. But then, Mama Pearl washes Bubba and then Beau. Now with the blankie soft and warm, dry from the clothesline, and Bubba and Beau clean and fresh smelling, their hearts are mended.

After reading aloud the text once through, discuss the text with your students. Work together to create a chart that describes the setting, characters, events, problem, and solution of the story. As an alternative, you could divide students into small groups to do this, or you may break up the topics and have one group address each aspect of a narrative.

Developing Ideas About Narratives Using Wordless Texts

In order to continue to refine your students' understanding of narrative as a genre, have your students write the stories for wordless texts. This experience provides your students with the opportunity to work individually or with a small group to write the story for a series of illustrations. This is an excellent precursor or scaffolding experience before you begin to write a story based upon photographs that you create or find.

There are a number of wordless picture books available for this purpose, and you'll want to have a selection of them. For example, I have been working with books by David Wiesner and Alexandra Day with my middle school students and with my university students (see Table 9; further information about each book can be found in the Appendix). You may find others that would be of interest to your students. Alexandra Day has written a series of wordless books in which she personifies a Rottweiler named Carl. In this series, Carl babysits the family child while mother goes out, goes shopping, runs errands, celebrates his birthday, takes the baby and a puppy to the park, and

Table 9
List of Suggested David Wiesner and Alexandra Day Wordless Picture Books
to Use for Identifying Elements in a Narrative

Day, A. (1991). *Good dog, Carl*. New York: Simon & Schuster.
Day, A. (1992). *Carl goes shopping*. New York: Farrar, Straus and Giroux.
Day, A. (1992). *Carl's afternoon in the park*. New York: Farrar, Straus and Giroux.
Day, A. (1992). *Carl's Christmas*. New York: Farrar, Straus and Giroux.
Day, A. (1995). *Carl goes to daycare*. New York: Farrar, Straus and Giroux.
Day, A. (1997). *Carl's birthday*. New York: Farrar, Straus and Giroux.
Day, A. (2005). *Carl's sleepy afternoon*. New York: Farrar, Straus and Giroux.
Wiesner, D. (1988). *Freefall*. New York: Scholastic.
Wiesner, D. (1990). *Hurricane*. Boston: Houghton Mifflin.
Wiesner, D. (1992). *June 29, 1999*. Boston: Houghton Mifflin.
Wiesner, D. (1997). *Tuesday*. Boston: Houghton Mifflin.
Wiesner, D. (2001). *The three pigs*. Boston: Houghton Mifflin.
Wiesner, D. (2006). *Flotsam*. Boston: Houghton Mifflin.

so on. Each of the books contains illustrations rich in detail. David Wiesner writes wordless texts based upon fantasies. For example, in *Freefall* (1988), a boy falls asleep while reading and visits a magical land where he can interact with chess pieces and dragons. Readers of *June 29, 1999* (1992), a book with minimal text, will meet Holly Evans, a third grader whose science experiment will bring giant vegetables into the world. *Flotsam* (2006) takes us to the shore where a boy who collects all the things that wash up on the beach finds an underwater camera that reveals the secrets of the deep.

First, choose a text and, as a class, study the first few images of the text. Then, have students talk through what they see, describing the way the elements look and how they are positioned. Next, demonstrate the process, working with the whole class to write the "story" for several pages. I like to write on the overhead projector or on a keyboard that can be projected to a screen where all can see. Doing it this way works best for me because I can make eye contact with my students while we are writing together. I can look to see who has an idea—and who might have one but may be reluctant to share. I also think it is helpful for students to see a visual example of how writers write and rewrite as they think. Together, you may decide to delete or move a paragraph or to move to an earlier place in the piece and add further description. Read aloud what you have written thus far. You may have individual students or small groups of students write the story for the rest of the images in this text, or you can continue to complete the story together as a class.

The following is a description of the first three illustrations in *Freefall* and an example of the text one of my classes and I wrote together. The words in italics are descriptions of the illustrations, and the words that follow are the narrative texts we wrote:

Illustration 1: A blond-haired boy, about 8 years old, is asleep in his wooden bed. The bedside table light is on, and the shade is cocked so the light shines on his face. His coverlet is a windowpane-check, wool blanket in various shades of green. In his arms he holds a black leather-bound book with gold trim. In bed with him is a wooden index-card box with a metal catch. The box is slightly open.

"Shhhhh, he's finally asleep," whispered Mrs. Golden. "Don't make a sound or you'll wake him!" Travis lay snug in the wooden bed that had belonged to his Uncle Phillip. He had fallen asleep while looking at the atlas. Earlier that evening they had received a call from the State Department. His Uncle Phillip was missing. His last known whereabouts were an island off the coast of South Africa. Travis had gone to bed with his atlas and his box of Uncle Phillip's chess pieces. He thought about how they used to play together whenever his uncle was home in Washington. He desperately wanted to find his uncle.

Illustration 2: The boy has turned on his side, his arm outstretched. The book has fallen open to reveal the pages of an atlas. The wooden box has opened to reveal what may be chess pieces. As our eyes move across the page, the blanket in shades of green becomes a bird's-eye view of fields bordered by puffy trees. A page of the atlas floats above these fields. Behind the boy the window of his room is open, and we can see the skyline of a city at night with a full moon rising from behind the buildings. His white curtains blow in the breeze.

Deep in the night when the full moon had risen over the city and a breeze arose and battered the curtains at his window, Travis fell into a deeper sleep. He moved restlessly in the wooden bed. His green checked coverlet fluttered, and the outer edge began to expand until it reached off into the distance, resting at the feet of a mountain range. The checks extended and elongated, becoming neatly divided plots of land bordered by rounded green trees and hedges. The leather atlas fell open, and a page from it drifted across the land and came to rest as if to mark a destination.

Illustration 3: The boy, still in his blue pajamas, stands in a checkerboard field. Several banners of different types flutter. He talks with a bishop and a lady-in-waiting. Approaching him are other people dressed in medieval dress. Some are attached to chess-piece bases. Others ride horses or walk. There are several creatures who do not look as if they are chess pieces but rather some sort of intermediaries. One wears a gray cap pulled down over his eyes and a full-length gray robe or trench coat.

Travis woke up to find himself standing in the middle of a checkerboard field, barefoot and wearing his blue pajamas. The field looked like those he had seen from airplanes, except that now the pieces were small—or he was a giant. Before he had time to look around him, Travis heard a rustling and sliding sound. Within moments he was surrounded by chess pieces as large as he. Some of the pieces had human figures atop the base. All were dressed elaborately as if they would have been the king and queens of ages past. Travis bowed silently to the queen who approached him. "Welcome to Checkerboard, young sir!" she exclaimed.

We continued on to write of the mysterious creatures standing beside Travis. We wrote of how Travis, sword and shield in hand, travels with them into a dark land and further still into the pages of a fairy tale in search of his Uncle Phillip. With each class group, the story is different. Even though we work from the same illustrations, our choices about character names and situations, problems, and solutions vary. Even the setting, though somewhat fixed by the illustrations, becomes different things to different writers.

For the next phase, provide a brief preview of the collection of wordless texts you have available for your students. Invite each student or group of students to look more carefully at the texts and then to choose one to use as the basis for a narrative. Provide each group with sheets of lined paper on which to write and remind them that they should break up the narrative so a single sheet of written text corresponds with a single illustration. Students who have computers or a computer lab available to them may choose to work there. Some students may want to create a PowerPoint presentation, scanning the illustrations and placing the text underneath. The level of complexity will depend upon the interests of your students and the resources you have available.

REFLECTION POINT

If you have not worked with picture books to develop concepts and do not have a collection of picture books, now might be a good time to team up with some of your fellow teachers and visit the local library. Sit and read together until you find a stack of picture books and wordless texts that you can use to help your students review, develop, and refine their ideas about narratives.

ACTIVITY 4

Writing Narratives With a Partner

Lamott (1995) states that "writing a first draft is very much like watching a Polaroid develop. You can't—and, in fact, you're not supposed to—know exactly what the picture is going to look like until it has finished developing" (p. 39). With classroom experiences that acknowledge this formative view of writing stories and provide various means of beginning and moving through the process of story writing, you can fuel the creativity of your students. Therefore, in the next activity, students will be writing narratives with a partner.

To get started, design prompts to help lead your students through the creation of a narrative. This experience provides students with a way of building upon their initial ideas about what is contained in a narrative through the previous activities. The following are suggested prompts for this purpose, although you may want to consider the strengths and needs of your students in order to adapt these prompts or create your own:

1. Write a brief description of a setting for a story.
2. Add and describe one character.
3. Add and describe a second character.
4. Describe a conflict between the two characters.
5. Have one character make a statement to the other to develop the conflict.
6. Let the second character respond.
7. Describe the two characters engaged in some action.
8. Write a brief dialogue between the characters.
9. Bring the situation to a climax.
10. Resolve the conflict.

Depending on the needs of your students, you may want to engage in a whole-class experience before you have them team up with a partner to write a narrative. You could do this by projecting the prompts and then talking and composing together as you make choices about your narrative. Then, once your students are ready, pair them up for narrative writing.

There are several ways you can have them address the prompts:

- You can read each one aloud and pause while students discuss and quick-write their ideas. Quick-writes are fast, focused writings.
- You can print the prompts on index cards and distribute them to groups one at a time as they complete each prompt (this enables you to visit briefly with the pair and check their progress).
- You can provide a list of prompts to each pair and enable them to do self-directed writing at their own pace.

The following is a sample of the type of narrative that you might expect from students at this stage based on the prompts (prompts appear above the response in italics):

Write a brief description of a setting for a story.
At a park with five friends playing basketball

Add and describe one character.
Shanteez is a boy who is quiet and sneaky.

Add and describe a second character.
Richard is a crybaby who always wants his way.

Describe a conflict between the two characters.
Shanteez told Richard he was "sorry" at basketball, and Richard told Shanteez *he* was the one who was "sorry" at basketball.

Have one character make a statement to the other to develop the conflict.
Shanteez said, "Let's play a game right now and see who's 'sorry'!"

Let the second character respond.
Richard replies, "I'm game!"

Describe the two characters engaged in some action.
Richard starts off the game, beating Shanteez 5 to 0. He starts to call Shanteez "sorry" again. They shove each other around a little, making faces.

Write a brief dialogue between the characters.
"You 'sorry'!"
"No, *you* 'sorry'!"
"Not as 'sorry' as you!"
"You the *'sorriest'*!"

Bring the situation to a climax.
Richard and Shanteez are at the end of the game. Richard says, "Boy, I will drop you."

Resolve the conflict.
Shanteez loses the game 12 to 0. He decides he is "sorry" at basketball and backs down.

You can see this as a first draft piece. Once the students have the framework established through this exercise, you can talk about how they might add details and description to help the reader have an enhanced sense of the setting. For instance, you can make suggestions for describing character movements, facial expressions, dress, and so on. You might discuss how dialogue between characters or the interior monologue of a character helps readers think about and understand the character's actions and motives. These aspects of the narrative could be developed in future sessions. With this experience you have helped your students visualize the various aspects of a narrative and the relationship between characters, action, and dialogue that take place in a story.

To extend this experience, read what the students have written and allow them to expand upon and revise through minilessons in setting, character, dialogue, and so on. You may also consider asking partners to share what they have written in a live Readers Theatre performance.

REFLECTION POINT

Think about how you might structure this experience for your own students. Would you use the same prompts, or is there a way to individualize the prompts based upon your students' needs and/or way of telling stories? Would you wait until the end to have students share, or do you think it would work better for your students to have a stop-and-share time after writing for each prompt?

ACTIVITY 5

On Our Own: Writing Narratives Individually

Now that your students have experienced a number of whole-group or partner studies of narratives, you can move to more complex and individualized writing experiences. Therefore, provide your students with opportunities to return to what they have learned about narratives and to build upon this knowledge as they write through the following activities: writing two-voice narratives based upon an encounter or situation and writing narratives based upon art reproductions or book illustrations.

Writing Two-Voice Narratives Based Upon an Encounter or Situation

I "discovered" what I call a two-voice narrative when reading Sandra Cisneros's novel *Caramelo* (2002), which chronicles the lives and passions of multiple generations of a Mexican American family. Within this novel, Cisneros writes in a number of different formats. She creates lists, writes poetry for two voices, includes a column for lonely hearts, tells us what can be learned about a person from the magazines they read, provides histories for processes like the making of rebozos, and so on. She also writes two-voice narratives. A two-voice narrative is a story told by two individuals. As Cisneros does it, the story is told at the same time as if the individuals are recalling the moments together and arguing about how it really was from different points of view. For example, Cisneros writes the following about Aunty Fina's home:

> It had withstood several centuries of epidemics, fires, earthquakes...with each age dividing its former elegance into tiny apartments....
> **Nonsense! It wasn't like that at all.... At the back of a narrow courtyard, up a flight of stairs, in the fourth doorway of a wide hallway Aunty Fina and her children lived. To get there, you first had to cross the open courtyard and pass under several archways....**
> That gave the building a bit of a Moorish feeling?
> **That gave the building a bit of a dreary feeling.** (p. 97)

Before you begin to write two-voice narratives with your students, you might want to read this six-page excerpt from the novel. Following the reading you can talk about how two or more people might view the same situation, place, or people in different ways.

It might also be helpful to view clips from films based upon books you are reading in class or selected scenes from other related films with your students and then to write or talk about how they view what is happening and how it makes them feel. Chances are you will have students who view one scene and come away from the viewing with three or four different impressions and sets of ideas about what they have seen. For example, when middle school students who are reading *The Outsiders* (Hinton, 1967) watch a clip from the film version, they come away with differing ideas about what has happened. We watched a clip of the greasers, Ponyboy, Johnny, and Dally, sitting in the stands behind Cherry, a cheerleader, and her friend Marcia at the movies. Dally talks roughly and teases Cherry. She ends up throwing a soft drink in his face. Some of the students saw this as an argument between the two, and others saw it as an instance in which they may actually be flirting with one another.

As an alternative you might ask pairs of students to take the place of two characters in the film clip and write a two-voice narrative of the incident or encounter from the characters' points of view. In this particular case, you could ask student pairs to write as Dally and Cherry, or as Ponyboy and Dally, or as Johnny and Dally. In each of these cases, the character pairs would "see" or "read" the encounter differently.

Once you have provided your students with an understanding of the process, you can invite them to think of possible encounters between two people or situations where they could "listen" to the views of two different people. For example, one of my university students, Larue, thought about the different views that she and her husband had about their son Matt playing high school football. The following is an excerpt selected from midway into her piece (the italicized type is her husband speaking and the roman type is Larue speaking; the bracketed type is what Larue is thinking but does not say aloud):

Look, Willowridge won the toss and Matt's running out onto the field with the defense.

Already!? I thought it would be a while before he went in. This is only his first varsity game. Couldn't they just let him sit on the bench and watch for a while?"

[Like maybe until February?]

Who is that lining up across from Matt? Is it that 300 pounder?

Oh, God, it is!

[Matt, just stop, drop, and roll like you learned in elementary school. When he starts coming at you, maybe he'll trip!]

Honey, just relax and uncover your eyes. He knows what to do. Go, Matt, get him!

[Easy for you to say, macho man!]

Just let me know when it's over.

When students have watched film clips and written as characters, or when they have written their own piece, invite students to read the pieces aloud.

There is nothing like hearing a two-voice narrative in a read-aloud—except perhaps hearing poems written for two voices! These pieces might be performed in a way similar to that for a reading of a poem for two voices.

REFLECTION POINT

I have written about using excerpts from *Caramelo* and film clips from *The Outsiders*. It is likely that you and your colleagues have discovered texts and films that would be meaningful to your students and would accomplish the same goals.

Work together with your team to identify a set of texts and film clips you can use for this purpose. Think about possible nonfiction or historical fiction works that can help your students build a greater awareness of various points of view during particular eras.

Writing Narratives Based Upon Art Reproductions or Book Illustrations

Have you ever stood in a museum looking at a painting or portrait and wondered what the subject or subjects would say if they could talk? What would their voice(s) sound like? You may not be able to take all of your students to the museum to contemplate the thoughts and voices of the subjects of paintings, but you can simulate the experience in your classrooms.

Begin with a study of the voices of various characters in young adult novels. Have students take notice of how different characters speak in ways that reveal something about themselves. Invite students to think about and talk about their own "voice" as writers. You may want to have students work in groups and share and reflect upon pieces they are currently writing, pieces they have written, or pieces in their writer's journals. Students should note and talk about what their peers are accomplishing in their writing. For example, a student might note that another student describes things in ways that are unusual and thought-provoking rather than resorting to the more common ways to describe something. As they work, students should point out specific places in the text where this is occurring. Because we are preparing to create a voice for a "character" in an art reproduction or book illustration, you may want to have the students in your groups focus on locating places where they hear their peers' voices.

Next, find art reproductions or book illustrations that you'd like your students to use as the basis for their writing. You could provide a number of art books and have your students choose among them, or you might focus on a single artist—I often use a book of Edward Hopper's paintings (Marker, 1990) with my classes. It's a good idea to make color copies of each work and laminate them for future use so students can choose a painting and take it to their desk to study, though if you are using multiple art reproduction books you can eliminate this step.

When everyone has chosen a painting, ask the students to spend five minutes looking at the image and then to write down everything they notice in their journal. You might have students show their images and talk to one another about what they notice. Once they have studied the visual aspects of the painting, they are ready to "listen" to the painting. They have already spent some time noticing the voice of characters in various novels and discovering their own voices, so the students are ready to try on the voice of someone else. Ask them to spend some silent time "listening" to the voice or voices in their painting and then to begin writing when they hear the characters begin to speak.

For example, one of my students, Joni, wrote the following about a Hopper painting ("Summertime," Marker, 1990, p. 109) of a beautiful woman in a filmy white dress standing on the steps of what looks like a courthouse or other public building:

> Out of the corner of my eye I can see Jim bounding up the steps. I am so nervous I can't look up for a moment. His suit fits him perfectly but does not suit him. My Jim looks at home casual with a shadow of a beard. Jim, my boyfriend, my future, stands before me in a taupe colored suit, white shirt, and tie. He is so clean shaven. I finally have the nerve to look him in the eyes and there he is...my Jim. His golden eyes smiling, fringed with blonde-tipped lashes. This is still Jim and then I realize it is still me. Just us, that is all....

Two other students, Isabel and Isidro, worked together on an image by Hopper of an elderly couple with a collie outside what looks like a remote farmhouse ("Cape Cod Evening," Marker, 1990, pp. 28–29). Their piece became a conversational narrative that they read aloud to us:

> "Ed, what's Mitzi lookin' at out there?"
>
> "I dunno, maybe the wind, she looks like she heard something."
>
> "What're you doing out here?"
>
> "I thought you were on the phone with Kevin."
>
> "Was...just came out to see what you were up to...are you okay, Ed?"
>
> "Yeah (sighs). I'm okay, I guess, I'm makin' it"
>
> "I know you're out here picking at the grass and thinking about Kevin."
>
> "Well, what if I am? A man's got a right to think about his son every now and then.... When are you gonna put dinner on the table, woman? I'm starving."
>
> "When I'm good and ready, Ed, pork chops'll be ready in a half hour or so...."

A younger student might write about this same image from the point of view of the dog, as follows:

> I wish they could run and play with me like Kevin used to do.
> When is he going to be home from college?

Why couldn't I go with him when he left?

I would have been a good dog.

I could have stayed in his room and waited for him to come home from school the way I used to do when he was younger and I was still a puppy.

I miss Kevin.

I miss running after the ball.

I miss playing chase with him.

I miss sleeping on the floor next to his bed.

Another student, Sandra, chose Hopper's well-known image of a late-night scene in a diner ("Nighthawks," Marker, 1990, pp. 86–87) and wrote about a waiter and a writer as follows:

"So what'll it be Mack?"

"I'll have a warm up on the coffee, thanks."

"No trouble. Not much action out there tonight?"

"Nope, it's pretty quiet...like there's nobody left living. Quiet as a tomb, quiet as the inside of a luxury car, quiet as a cloud drifting by."

"Oh, Mack. You're such a kidder. You even talk like a writer when you're off work."

"Well, Dave, you've got to live every moment as a writer—think like a writer, dream like a writer, get inside the sheer being of being a writer—that's what it's all about. Not a second goes by that I'm not writing or thinking about writing, finishing a piece, revising, so on. Why you know, I've even got my journal right here with me now. I think I'll write about this...."

After students complete their narratives, have them share their work through read-alouds. You will likely discover that students are able to "hear" the voices in the paintings, and students will discover that dialogue can be a powerful element of a narrative.

ACTIVITY 6

Writing Narratives Based Upon Personal Photographs

Where do we get our ideas for a story? We might witness an event as we drive to and from work. We might read something in a book and wonder, "What if?" We might think about something that has happened to us. I have also found that you can get ideas for a story from a series of photographs. These might be photographs that we pull from magazines, photographs culled from our family albums or picture boxes, or even photographs we stage and take specifically for the purpose of writing.

Talk to your students about how writers might get ideas for their narratives. You may want to share these aforementioned ideas with them, and something I like to share with my students is Walter Dean Myers's ideas connecting photography and writing. I remember listening to author Walter Dean Myers speak at a National Council of Teachers of English conference about his process of writing. He told us that he walked the streets in his neighborhood carrying a camera. When he saw the places he wanted to include in his novel, he photographed them. While he was walking, he also took photographs of people he encountered. And he tore pictures of people from magazines. These people might become the characters in his novel. As he collected the photographs, he taped them to the walls of the room where he wrote. Then, as he wrote, he would be surrounded by his setting and his characters.

Getting Started—Finding Your Way Together

First, choose a number of photographs from magazines and reproduce them on transparencies, or you may prefer to work with your own photographs, projecting them where the entire class can see. You might also ask your students to donate a photo or two and then choose several from these to work with.

As always, it is best to begin with a whole-class experience of the process. Begin by looking at each photograph together. For example, in one of my classes, I shared photographs depicting the following images:

- A blue dollhouse sized cottage in a garden
- Croquet mallets and wickets propped up against a tree
- A group of people making funny faces and posing together for a photo on the beach
- A white horse with blue eyes
- A smiling man sitting in a chair
- A man looking off into the distance with a pen in his hand
- A woman, dressed in a suit, holding a baby in the air
- A gray-haired man sitting on a couch in a mysteriously ornamental room
- A male and female that are half human, half fish swimming together

I projected the photographs and we talked for a few moments about each one.

You will want to do the same with your photographs. After the discussion, lay the photographs on a large table in the center of the room and ask everyone to come to the table with their journals. Spend a few moments having students stand shoulder to shoulder writing their impressions of a few of the photographs, which will read like the beginning or pieces of a story. Allow enough time for students to write about two to three photographs. The objective is for students to write a narrative based upon several of the photographs, so they will want to be working to tie the photographs together in some way. If you want to include details, descriptions, dialogue, and so forth, you shouldn't ask your students to write about more than a few photographs. For the first exercise though, it is a good idea to have a variety of pictures so students have a choice.

Once your students have had an opportunity to study a photograph or two and write for a few minutes, ask for volunteers to share something that they have written. The work will be unpolished at this point, but the idea is to get a feel for how it is going and what others are thinking. For example, one of my students, Janet, shared the following piece she wrote about the croquet set:

> The croquet set sat among the oak trees near the mysterious cottage that was said to be enchanted, or some say, bewitched. The croquet set belongs to Mr. Belle, Anne Marie's father. He was full of mysteries.

Another student, Darry, wrote the following about the same photo:

> Setting: A coastal town somewhere in Spain. This is George. He is the head of the family. He lives with his family in a house deep in the woods. His oldest son, Josh, is a fantasy writer. Josh is currently writing a story about a merman and a mermaid who are searching for their baby mermaid. Josh's wife is a judge in town. They both have an adorable baby girl that they love very much. On the weekends, Josh and Judy love to ride horses and play croquet. Afterwards Judy tends the garden while Josh builds the baby a playhouse. Soon the relatives will come over to celebrate the baby's first birthday.

At the end of the day or class period, ask students to come to the next class meeting with a series of their own photographs. Students may take their own photographs, pull pictures from magazines, make copies of pictures from family albums, or bring in a combination of all three. If students have access to computers, you may want to have them create printouts of their digital photos with lined spaces beside each one for writing, using the lined area to draft their ideas (as you will see one of my students, Juan, doing in the next section).

On Their Own: Individualizing the Process

When your class meets the next day, the students should have their photographs and be ready to write. Have them begin by talking to a partner about the photographs they brought in. This helps students begin to "discover" what they have and the stories that may be inside the photographs. For example, my student Udalia showed another student, Randi, a photograph of a frail old woman standing in a clearing of the woods. Behind her is a bench made from an overturned bucket with a rough board on top. Hanging from a large tree is an aluminum foil pan and other kitchen items. Udalia explained,

> This is my great grandmother. She was 103 years old when this picture was taken. She raised my grandmother. My grandmother's [biological] parents died of tuberculosis and so she raised her. She raised a lot of kids, but none of them were biologically her kids. This picture was taken after her house burnt down. She had to stay with my grandmother, and my grandmother was real fussy and she made my great grandmother feel uncomfortable in her house. My great grandmother was used to working in the fields—so here, between the house and the woods she made an area for herself. She has her garden out here, her teacups are hung on a line like clothes. In the background, you see these roses? I cut a piece from one of these roses and took it home so we could plant it in our yard. It's growing there now, and my parents and I think of her every time we look at it. She told me to plant it in a hole with dry beans and it took just like that. Now it's a beautiful bush growing all over the fence by the driveway....

Another student, Juan, created printouts of his digital photos with lined spaces beside each one for writing, using the lined area to draft his ideas. Pointing to a close-up photo of a hibiscus flower, he told me, "As the flower blooms that's the way I feel living here with my parents. This is a good place for us to be." Another student, Demetria, explained that she planned to begin by writing about each character, saying, "Once I get to know them, I'll know what the story is going to be about." Michelle, like many of the students, decided that it is difficult for her to make up a new story about photographs of friends and family. Because she wanted to test her inventiveness, she mixed photographs from magazines with her own pictures. Yulna numbered her photographs with sticky notes and wrote short phrases on each note. These examples show that each student may have a unique method of working that helps them begin to think about their photographs and the stories they want to write.

The response of younger students will be much the same. As they order their photographs and perhaps interject pictures from magazines, they will move images of characters and representations of events back and forth until they are ready to write. For example, the following is a piece a younger student might write about a picture of a turtle and a beach cut from a magazine and photographs of herself and her father:

> Sammy was a Mississippi Mud Turtle. Somehow he had gotten himself out of the mud and onto the beach. He was waving his turtle arms around and trying to dig himself deep into the sand where it would be cooler when he felt a shadow cover him. It was a girl and her father. He could hear her begging her father to let her take him home with her. "Please daddy, can I take this turtle home with me? Ginny has a fish and Tod has a hamster. I need a pet too."

REFLECTION POINT

Spend a week or two observing your students to notice what they do when faced with new learning and unfamiliar tasks. Can you use your observations of the way your students learn/work to help you design methods and demonstrations that will enhance your students' learning?

Do you think it would help to set aside time for students to share their processes with others?

Writing and Sharing the Photo-Based Narratives

Now that students have developed their initial ideas for their narrative, they can begin writing. You will want to devote several class periods to writing and periodic sharing, because it will be helpful for students to see and hear what others are writing as they work on their own pieces. When the students have completed their narratives, have them share their work.

For example, one of my students, Annalyn, has written the following narrative beneath a photograph she has made of a large, colorful mural looming over a town square in Mexico (see Figure 25):

Figure 25
Annalyn's Photo of Mural to Accompany Narrative

Isabella and Marcos were very much in love. In the little pueblo of Doneraki everyone knew who they were because they always walked the streets hand in hand. They were inseparable. They even made a living together as street performers. Marcos was a very talented guitarist, while Isabella was a beautiful dancer. Every day they walked to the plaza in the heart of the city. Marcos would play an enchanting tune and Isabella would dance around him twirling her bright colored skirt in circles and stamping her feet on the concrete. Sometimes they made a lot, sometimes they made a little, but they always had food on the table and an unbreakable bond between them....

Another student, Nekisha, wrote the following narrative about a series of photographs she took that show us the silhouettes of two men and a sunrise bursting through dark, ominous clouds over the ocean (see Figure 26):

The harbor was lined with boats ready to sail the deep and dark waters. John and Mark were standing along the deck admiring the sunrise. They talked and placed a bet on who was going to catch the biggest fish. They had waited all week to go deep sea fishing. As they boarded the boat they realized the water was rather still and quiet. It was pretty quiet around the harbor itself, which made Mark a little nervous. As the boat eased away from the dock seagulls flew overhead looking for something to eat. Mark and John could

Figure 26
Nekisha's Photo of Sun and Clouds to Accompany Narrative

feel the slight coolness of the wind as it hit their faces.... Two hours into the sea, the boat engine stopped and the anchor dropped. Mark and John knew this would be the spot where they would catch their biggest fish.... Suddenly the sky began to darken. Heavy clouds rolled in with a fierce rage. The wind picked up. In the distance Mark could see a rain storm coming their way. The waves started to gain strength, almost engulfing the craft. Mark grabbed on to the rail and held on for his dear life. The wind was plowing against his face....

A younger student might write the following narrative about a photo of his dog:

This is my dog, Bart. As you can see Bart is a pretty big, hairy, black dog. He is smiling in this picture. He smiles a lot. Bart is like a member of our family. He pretty much goes everywhere with us. He has his own place in the back seat of the car. He likes to hang his head out the window and try to take bites out of the wind. I like to take Bart with me when we go to the park. He never gets tired of playing around. His favorite thing is to run after an old ball. Well, maybe his second favorite. His first favorite is to jump into the pond and go for a swim. Come to think about it, Bart and I are a lot alike. I like to ride in the car and stick my head out too. I like to play ball, and best of all I like to dive in the pond. Maybe that's why Bart and I are friends. We have a lot in common.

During this activity, the most important aspects for students seem to be the time to share and talk about their photographs before writing *and* the time to write and share while working together in the classroom. Each time I looked up from my own writing, students were deeply engaged in what they were doing and pens and pencils were flying across the page in a way I had not seen before. As one of my students, Charlene, noted after listening to several students share what they were writing and then later sharing her piece in progress, "At first I was just writing and it wasn't even a story.... NOW, I've got a story going, and I can't wait to write about what happens next!"

Conclusion

At the beginning of this chapter I wrote about a photograph of my mother as a young girl. As I examined the elements within the photograph I tried to imagine what had happened in the moments before and what would happen in the moments to follow. As I let myself imagine, a story began to unfold.

Our lives are a series of stories. Each story has a beginning and an end, a sequence of events, a problem, and a solution. Each story is populated with characters. As we move through life we "collect" stories. In her novel *Sea Glass*, Anita Shreve (2002) writes about a character, Honoria, who collects a piece of sea glass every morning when she walks on the beach. Each piece of sea glass has a significance and a story for Honoria.

While the sea glass imparts a story to Honoria, we look to photographs to inspire and support our students in the writing of narratives. In this chapter we examined and analyzed images as an aspect of visual literacy, looking at how our prior knowledge and experiences color the way we view and respond to visual images. We worked with our students to identify and clarify the elements of narrative and then wrote the stories for picture books without words. This experience helped our students begin to write the stories for images assembled by others. We invited our students to write guided and two-voice narratives so they could explore the dimensions of storytelling. They expanded upon this further as they wrote based upon reproductions of paintings. Finally, students constructed or collected their own series of images and used these to inform their writing of a narrative. As this occurred, students created visual referents and guideposts for their stories.

Experiences such as these enable our students to refine the art of narrative as they carefully construct characters and settings inspired by visual images. The images are the inspiration, and the combining and rearranging of the images enables the writer to physically manipulate the narrative before or during the act of writing. When we engage our students in experiences such as these, we are enhancing their visual and critical literacy skills and then setting them free to imagine what happens next.

REFERENCES

Alvermann, D.E., & Hagood, M.C. (2000). Critical media literacy: Research, theory, and practice in "new times." *Journal of Educational Research, 93*, 193–205.

Alvermann, D.E., Moon, J.S., & Hagood, M.C. (1999). *Popular culture in the classroom: Teaching and researching critical media literacy*. Newark, DE: International Reading Association.

Barrett, T. (2003). Interpreting visual culture. *Art Education, 56*(2), 6–12.

Barthes, R. (1977). Rhetoric of the image. In S. Heath (Ed. & Trans.), *Image, music, text* (pp. 32–51). New York: Hill & Wang.

Garrett-Petts, W.F. (2000). Garry Disher, Michael Ondaatje, and the haptic eye: Taking a second look at print literacy. *Children's Literature in Education, 31*, 39–52.

Hamilton, M. (2000). Expanding the new literacy studies: Using photographs to explore literacy as a social practice. In D. Barton, M. Hamilton, & R. Ivanic (Eds.), *Situated literacies: Reading and writing in context* (pp. 16–34). New York: Routledge.

Lamott, A. (1995). *Bird by bird: Some instructions on writing and life*. New York: Anchor.

Library of Congress Prints and Photographs Online Catalog. Image of a Chinese child with an adult on step outside of building, Chinatown, New York City. Part of the George Grantham Bain Collection. Retrieved October 26, 2007, from hdl.loc.gov/loc.pnp/cph.3c20168

Nodelman, P. (1991). The eye and the I: Identification and first-person narratives in picture books. *Children's Literature, 19*, 1–30.

Westcott, W. (1997). Picture writing and photographic techniques for the writing process. *English Journal, 86*(7), 49–54.

LITERATURE CITED

Appelt, K. (2002). *Bubba and Beau, best friends*. San Diego, CA: Harcourt.

Banyai, I. (1995a). *Re-zoom*. New York: Puffin.

Banyai, I. (1995b). *Zoom*. New York: Puffin.

Cisneros, S. (2002). *Caramelo*. New York: Knopf.

Hinton, S.E. (1967). *The outsiders*. New York: Dell.

Marker, S. (1990). *Edward Hopper*. New York: Crown.

Shreve, A. (2002). *Sea glass*. Boston: Little, Brown.

Wiesner, D. (1988). *Freefall*. New York: Scholastic.

Wiesner, D. (1992). *June 29, 1999*. Boston: Houghton Mifflin.

Wiesner, D. (2006). *Flotsam*. Boston: Houghton Mifflin.

What to Read: Featuring Photographs

This appendix offers a selection of annotated bibliographies for the picture books, young adult literature, poetry books, short stories, and other works that were used with the activities in this book and that relate to the importance of photographs. These works can be used to stimulate thinking and reflection specific to the chapter topics presented. Information about each work includes a brief summary as well as notations about genre, how the material might be used, and grade level of interest. A key to the notation codes is included at the bottom of each page.

Each entry begins with a citation of the book, followed by a brief summary and then a codes list in parentheses. The first group of letter codes within the parentheses refers to the genre of the book: novel (N), young adult novel (YA), picture book (PB), poetry (P), memoir (M), biography (B), short story (SS), or informational text (IT). The second group of letter codes within the parentheses refers to the best use for the text, whether it be teacher background information (TBI), teacher and student read-aloud (TSRA), student independent reading (SIR), or student research and background information (SRBI). The third group of codes—a number code—refers to the grade level in which this text might appropriately be used for the purposes I have described in the book. Please note that this number code does not refer to the reader level of the text. In some cases, I have also included a brief notation indicating texts with which teacher excerpts would be best used for students in grades 4 through 8, while students in grades 9 through 12 could read the book in its entirety.

Introduction
Reading and Writing About Photographs in Grades 4–12

MacLachlan, P. (1991). *Journey*. New York: Delacorte.

> This moving chapter book is about a boy named Journey who loses his mother and his family photographs. Journey's grandfather, grandmother, and sister, Cat, show him how to take pictures, how to see life for what it is, and how to regain his joy. (YA; TSRA, SIR; 4–12)

Chapter 1
Remembering Meaningful Moments:
Reading Photographs to Write Memoirs

Auster, P. (1988). *The invention of solitude*. New York: Penguin.

> In this memoir, Paul Auster collects his thoughts on fatherhood. In the first part of the book, he writes of the death of his father and reflects on his relationship with him. In the second part of the book, he writes about his own role as a father and what it means to be a writer. (M; TBI, TSRA; 8–12)

Burandt, H., & Dale, S. (1997). *Tales from the homeplace: Adventures of a Texas farm girl*. New York: Henry Holt.

> This delightful collection of nine memoirs is about the life of a Texas girl growing up on a cotton farm in the 1930s. These stories are based on the life of Harriet Burandt's mother, Irene Hutto. Remarkable Irene saves her brothers and sisters from a wild panther, saves an aging horse from the glue factory, and helps us see how life might have been during this tumultuous time. (M, SS; TSRA, SIR; 4–12)

Cisneros, S. (2002). *Caramelo*. New York: Knopf.

> This book is a multigenerational story of a Mexican American family. We travel with the Reyes family on their annual car trip from Chicago to Mexico City. As we move back and forth in time, between Chicago; Mexico City; and San Antonio, Texas, we come to know the family history—sometimes real and sometimes not so real! Teachers could read aloud excerpts, or more mature readers could read on their own. (N, M; TSRA, SIR; 9–12)

Creech, S. (2000). *Fishing in the air*. New York: Joanna Cotler Books.

> *Fishing in the Air* is a beautiful picture book illustrated by Chris Raschka. Sharon Creech writes about a father who takes his son on a fishing trip to "catch the air" and "catch the breeze." This is a father who notes that the streetlamps in the early morning are "glowing like tiny moons all in a row" and tells his son that once his own father had taught him to fish in the river near the tiny gray house where he lived—a gray house with a red roof that "looked like a little box with a red hat." (PB, M; TSRA, SIR; 4–12)

The parenthetical information at the end of each annotation indicates the material's genre, the best use for the material, and appropriate grade range. *Genres*: N = novel, YA = young adult novel, PB = picture book, P = poetry, M = memoir, B = biography, SS = short story, IT = informational text. *Best Use*: TBI = teacher background information, TSRA = teacher and student read-aloud, SIR = student independent reading, SRBI = student research and background information.

Giff, P.R. (2002). *Pictures of Hollis Woods*. New York: Random House.

Hollis Woods is a 12-year-old girl who has lived in foster homes all her life. Many of the chapters begin with a description of a picture Hollis has drawn or created. The pictures help her remember her life with the Regans, a foster family she feels she may never return to. As Hollis struggles to build a life of her own, her creativity and her longing for a family will keep her focused on accomplishing that goal. (YA; TSRA, SIR; 5–12)

Hart, E.T. (1999). *Barefoot heart: Stories of a migrant child*. Tempe, AZ: Bilingual Press.

Elva Trevino Hart was born in south Texas to Mexican immigrants. With this memoir she tells us of the history of her family and of the day-to-day events in her life—the life of a child growing up in a family of migrant farm workers and learning to move beyond the cruelty of those who do not understand her life or her language. This memoir reflects on family, love, life, and attaining dreams!.(M; TSRA, SIR; 4–8 [teacher-selected excerpts], 9–12 [whole book])

Houston, G. (1992). *My great-aunt Arizona*. New York: HarperCollins.

My Great-Aunt Arizona takes us back to times gone by. The words of Gloria Houston and the illustrations of Susan Condie Lamb let us "see" what it might have been like to be a teacher in a one-room schoolhouse long ago. Arizona loved to read, and she dreamed of going to far away places. She never left the Blue Ridge Mountains. Instead she became a teacher, built a school, planted flowers in the window, and left a legacy of love and a thirst for learning to the many generations of children she taught. (PB, M; TSRA, SIR; 4–12)

Ingold, J. (1998). *Pictures, 1918*. New York: Harcourt Brace.

It is just before World War I, and someone has set Asia's barn on fire. She longs for a camera, an Autographic, so she can take pictures that could make a difference—pictures of her now lost rabbit, Straw Bit; pictures of her friend Nick before he goes off to war; and pictures to capture the life that seems to be slipping away and changing every day. (YA; TSRA, SIR; 4–12)

MacLachlan, P. (1991). *Three names*. New York: HarperCollins.

Sumptuous watercolors by Alexander Pertzoff illustrate this beautiful story by Patricia MacLachlan. This is the story of Great Grandfather and his dog, Three Names, who lived on the prairie long ago. MacLachlan's words give readers a sense of the passage of seasons and events as a young boy and his dog go to school in a one-room schoolhouse. This story is rich with details such as playing marbles in the meadow, having Three Names sleep on his feet in school, and celebrating the last day of school when everyone comes in white starched shirts. (PB, M; TSRA, SIR; 4–12)

Mora, P. (1997). *Tomás and the library lady*. New York: Knopf.

Written by Pat Mora and illustrated by Raul Colon, this picture book is a memoir of the life of Tomás Rivera, who became the chancellor of the University of California

---

The parenthetical information at the end of each annotation indicates the material's genre, the best use for the material, and appropriate grade range. *Genres*: N = novel, YA = young adult novel, PB = picture book, P = poetry, M = memoir, B = biography, SS = short story, IT = informational text. *Best Use*: TBI = teacher background information, TSRA = teacher and student read-aloud, SIR = student independent reading, SRBI = student research and background information.

at Riverside. *Tomás and the Library Lady* depicts his life as a young boy—a time when he traveled from Texas to Iowa in the summer with his family to work in the fields. Tomás loves the stories of his grandfather, but when it seems that he knows them all, Tomás's grandfather sends him to the library to find other stories in books. Tomás is befriended by the librarian and spends the summer reading and sharing stories with the librarian and with his family. (PB, M; TSRA, SIR; 4–12)

Ringgold, F. (1993). *Dinner at Aunt Connie's house*. New York: Hyperion Books for Children.

Faith Ringgold's painted story quilt "The Dinner Quilt" is transformed in this picture book. Melody and her family get together every summer at the home of her Aunt Connie and Uncle Bates. Every year, Aunt Connie, an artist, unveils a wonderful meal and a new collection of paintings. This year the paintings are of 12 strong African American women, women like Marian Anderson, Zora Neale Hurston, and Sojourner Truth...and most surprising of all, the paintings can talk! Together with Melody and her newly adopted cousin, Lonnie, we "listen" to the lives of these inspiring women. (PB, M; TSRA, SIR; 4–12)

Taulbert, C.L. (1989). *Once upon a time when we were colored*. New York: Penguin.

Clifton Taulbert writes of his childhood in the segregated south of the 1950s. Taulbert was raised by aunts, uncles, cousins, neighbors, and friends who were strong and loving and who instilled in him a sense of pride in his heritage and a belief that dreams could come true. (M; TSRA, SIR; 4–8 [teacher-selected excerpts], 9–12 [whole book])

Watts, J.H. (1997). *Keepers*. New York: Lee & Low.

Kenyon, a young boy, wants to be the keeper for his family, but his grandmother, Little Dolly, tells him that the honor must go to a female. As we read further we see Kenyon talking about his grandmother with the antique dealer, the carriage driver for tourists, and the caretaker at the cemetery. Each one of them has a story to tell about Little Dolly. Kenyon decides to collect these stories and give them to his grandmother on her 90th birthday in a handmade book. (PB, M; TSRA, SIR; 4–12)

Wolff, T. (1989). *This boy's life: A memoir*. New York: Grove Press.

Compared by the *Philadelphia Inquirer* to both *Great Expectations* and *Huckleberry Finn*, *This Boy's Life* is the story of a boy being raised by a single mother in the 1950s. Toby and his mother are forever moving, and Toby must fight to define himself and make himself a place in each new "home." He does this with humor and tenacity in a heart-warming and humorous tale of boyhood. (M; TSRA, SIR; 4–8 [teacher-selected excerpts], 9–12 [whole book])

Yardley, J. (1991). *The red ball*. New York: Harcourt Brace Jovanovich.

Joanie, trying to retrieve her red ball from her dog Max, ventures into the attic where she finds a box of old family photographs. As she looks at each photograph, she sees her red ball in the hands of people from the past. Eventually, Joanie finds herself inside the photographs—chasing the red ball and learning about the life of her grand-

---

The parenthetical information at the end of each annotation indicates the material's genre, the best use for the material, and appropriate grade range. *Genres*: N = novel, YA = young adult novel, PB = picture book, P = poetry, M = memoir, B = biography, SS = short story, IT = informational text. *Best Use*: TBI = teacher background information, TSRA = teacher and student read-aloud, SIR = student independent reading, SRBI = student research and background information.

mother, the first owner of the red ball. Written and illustrated by Joanna Yardley, this is a fascinating book in which each picture "photograph" provides a clue. (PB, M; TSRA, SIR; 4–12)

Zinsser, W. (Ed.). (1987). *Inventing the truth: The art and craft of memoir*. Boston: Houghton Mifflin.

This is a wonderful collection of memoirs and excerpts from a question-and-answer session that originated as a series of talks given at the New York Public Library. Six American writers were invited to discuss the art of recapturing memories and writing a memoir. These authors are Annie Dillard, Toni Morrison, Russell Baker, Alfred Kazin, Lewis Thomas, and William Zinsser. (M, SS; TBI, TSRA; 8–12)

Chapter 2
Understanding the Who and the Why:
Reading Photographs to Write About Ourselves

Bambara, T.C. (1992). *Gorilla, my love*. New York: Vintage Contemporaries.

Author Toni Cade Bambara begins this book with a humorous introduction about why she made up the stories in this book rather than use events or people in her life as inspiration. Included in this collection are 16 short stories such as "Raymond's Run," "The Lesson," "Sweet Town," "Maggie of the Green Bottles," and "The Johnson Girls." (SS; TSRA, SIR; 6–12)

Buzzeo, T. (2002). *The sea chest*. New York: Dial Books for Young Readers.

A worn photograph prompts Maita to tell her niece about her life growing up in a lighthouse on an island off the coast of Maine. Maita, her mother, and her father, the lighthouse keeper, are the only inhabitants of the island. One morning after a raging storm, Maita and her father discover a sea chest wrapped in blankets. Inside is a baby they will raise as Maita's sister. (PB; TSRA; 4–12)

Cisneros, S. (1984). *The house on Mango Street*. New York: Random House.

Cisneros writes a collection of stories that are each several pages in length. Titles such as "My Name," "Meme Ortiz," "Those Who Don't," "Edna's Ruthie," and "Mango Says Goodbye Sometimes" represent the lives of colorful characters that many of our students will be able to relate to and talk about. (SS; TSRA, SIR; 6–12)

Fleischman, P. (1997). *Seedfolks*. New York: HarperCollins.

A vacant lot in an inner-city neighborhood of high rises becomes a site of renewal for 13 diverse individuals. Each of the 13 tells us his or her story in a chapter. As we read about them as separate people, we watch them grow together through their efforts to create a garden, meeting place, and something of beauty in the vacant lot. (YA; TSRA, SIR; 4–12)

The parenthetical information at the end of each annotation indicates the material's genre, the best use for the material, and appropriate grade range. *Genres*: N = novel, YA = young adult novel, PB = picture book, P = poetry, M = memoir, B = biography, SS = short story, IT = informational text. *Best Use*: TBI = teacher background information, TSRA = teacher and student read-aloud, SIR = student independent reading, SRBI = student research and background information.

Franco, B. (Ed.). (2001). *Things I have to tell you: Poems and writing by teenage girls*. Cambridge, MA: Candlewick.

Editor Betty Franco contacted girls ages 12 through 18 through their English teachers, teen magazines, and other means. She invited them to write about what they thought about and how they felt. Photographer Nina Nickles worked with community volunteers, principals, psychologists, and others to find the young women who would allow her to see inside their lives and photograph them for the book. This book serves as an honest and sometimes painful portrait of what it means to be young and female. (P, M, SS; TSRA, SIR; 7–12)

Gallo, D.R. (Ed.). (1984). *Sixteen short stories by outstanding writers for young adults*. New York: Delacorte.

This book contains 16 short stories about friendship, turmoil, love, decisions, and families. Stories by authors such as Norma Fox Mazer, Richard Peck, M.E. Kerr, Joan Aiken, and Robert Cormier are included. (SS; TSRA, SIR; 6–12)

Gallo, D.R. (Ed.). (1989). *Connections: Short stories by outstanding writers for young adults*. New York: Delacorte.

This book contains 17 short stories about encounters, clashes, surprises, and insights. Stories by authors such as Sue Ellen Bridgers, Gordon Korman, Robin Brancato, Tod Strasser, Jerry Spinelli, and Ouida Sebestyen are included. (SS; TSRA, SIR; 6–12)

Giff, P.R. (2002). *Pictures of Hollis Woods*. New York: Random House.

Hollis Woods is a 12-year-old girl who has lived in foster homes all her life. Many of the chapters begin with a description of a picture Hollis has drawn or created. The pictures help her remember her life with the Regans, a foster family she feels she may never return to. As Hollis struggles to build a life of her own, her creativity and her longing for a family will keep her focused on accomplishing that goal. (YA; TSRA, SIR; 5–12)

Kendrick, R. (2005). *Revealing character: Texas tintypes*. Albany, TX: Bright Sky Press.

Photographer Robb Kendrick traveled across Texas to meet and photograph hundreds of modern-day working cowboys and cowgirls. He captured their images in tintypes, a photographic method that dates back to the 1800s. Pages filled with the images and words of these unique individuals give readers a feeling of their spirit and drive and their love of the land. (IT; TSRA, SIR, SRBI; 4–12)

MacLachlan, P. (1991). *Journey*. New York: Delacorte.

This moving chapter book is about a boy named Journey who loses his mother and his family photographs. Journey's grandfather, grandmother, and sister, Cat, show him how to take pictures, how to see life for what it is, and how to regain his joy. (YA; TSRA, SIR; 4–12)

Polacco, P. (2002). *When lightning comes in a jar*. New York: Philomel Books.

Patricia Polacco tells stories of her family reunions—joyful times in which cousins, aunts, and uncles gathered for picnics with jello salads and meat loaves, times when they played

---

The parenthetical information at the end of each annotation indicates the material's genre, the best use for the material, and appropriate grade range. *Genres*: N = novel, YA = young adult novel, PB = picture book, P = poetry, M = memoir, B = biography, SS = short story, IT = informational text. *Best Use*: TBI = teacher background information, TSRA = teacher and student read-aloud, SIR = student independent reading, SRBI = student research and background information.

baseball and croquet and had brown-sack races, times when her grandmother and aunts looked at old family photographs and told stories about riding in the first motorcar, seeing the first airplane, and catching lightning bugs in a jar. (PB; TSRA, SIR; 4–12)

Rochman, H., & McCampbell, D.Z. (Eds.). (1993). *Who do you think you are? Stories of friends and enemies.* Boston: Little, Brown.

Seventeen short stories by authors Ray Bradbury, John Updike, Carson McCullers, Maya Angelou, and others are included in this book. These stories focus on a multitude of different friendships, showing us how we make, keep, and sometimes lose our friends. (SS; TSRA, SIR; 6–12)

Solomon, B.H., & Panetta, E. (Eds.). (2004). *Once upon a childhood: Stories and memoirs of American youth.* New York: New American Library.

This book is a collection of memoirs and/or short stories by authors such as Julia Alvarez, Alice Hoffman, Rebecca Walker, Sandra Cisneros, Tobias Wolff, Frank Conroy, and Jack London. Because of the graphic and sexual nature of some of the memoirs/stories, teachers will need to choose carefully what they share. (M, SS; TBI, TSRA, SIR; 10–12)

Soto, G. (1990). *Baseball in April and other stories.* New York: Harcourt Brace.

This book of short stories written by Gary Soto is a recollection of his own youth in California and is about resourceful, funny, honest Latino kids who confront issues related to relationships and survival. Included in this collection are "The No Guitar Blues," "Seventh Grade," "The Karate Kid," "La Bamba," and others. (SS; TSRA, SIR; 4–12)

Walker, R. (2001). *Black, white, and Jewish: Autobiography of the shifting self.* New York: Riverhead Books.

With this memoir, Rebecca Walker, the daughter of Alice Walker, the author of *The Color Purple* and other memorable books, and Mel Leventhal, a white Jewish civil rights activist and lawyer, frankly writes about her struggle against discrimination, her search for her identity, and her exploration of sexuality. (M; TSRA, SIR; 4–8 [teacher-selected excerpts], 9–12 [whole book])

Chapter 3
Creating Biographies With Voice:
Reading Photographs to Write About People

Appelt, K., & Schmitzer, J.C. (2001). *Down Cut Shin Creek: The pack horse librarians of Kentucky.* New York: HarperCollins.

This informational text chronicles the Kentucky Pack Horse Library Project in words and photographs. While many of the Works Progress Administration projects during the U.S. Great Depression provided work for men, this is one of the few jobs directed toward women. The close of the coal mines due to factory shutdowns and the Ohio River flood, which washed away fertile topsoil, left many Kentuckians

---

The parenthetical information at the end of each annotation indicates the material's genre, the best use for the material, and appropriate grade range. *Genres:* N = novel, YA = young adult novel, PB = picture book, P = poetry, M = memoir, B = biography, SS = short story, IT = informational text. *Best Use:* TBI = teacher background information, TSRA = teacher and student read-aloud, SIR = student independent reading, SRBI = student research and background information.

destitute. This is the story of the librarians who packed up reading materials and traveled by horse or mule to visit these people where they lived. (IT; SIR, SRBI; 4–12)

Brown, M.W. (1949). *The important book*. New York: HarperCollins.

This collection of poems by Margaret Wise Brown, the author of *Goodnight Moon*, features short pieces that focus on the important aspects of everyday things such as grass, snow, the wind, a spoon, and a daisy. (PB, P; TSRA, SIR; 4–12)

Hesse, K. (1999). *Come on rain!* New York: Scholastic.

A young girl in the inner city eagerly waits for rain. When it comes, she and her friends and their mothers dance in the streets, celebrating life and renewal. Beautiful watercolors illustrate the vivid, figurative language in the book. (PB; TSRA, SIR; 4–12)

Keenan, S. (1996). *Scholastic encyclopedia of women in the United States*. New York: Scholastic.

Short one- to two-page articles about American women from the 1500s to the 1990s, with chapters divided by decade, comprise this book. Each article is accompanied by a black-and-white photograph of the featured individual. Of particular interest are the diverse representations of women and the inclusion of many notable individuals who students may not be familiar with. (IT; SIR, SRBI; 4–12)

Levine, K. (2002). *Hana's suitcase: A true story*. Morton Grove, IL: Albert Whitman.

This informational text, which includes photographs, takes us into two worlds. We travel with Fumiko Ishioka, curator of the Holocaust Education Center in Tokyo, Japan, while she searches for information about Hana Brady, the former owner of a suitcase that arrived at the museum in 2000. Our journey takes us back to the 1930s— first to Nove Mesto, Czechoslovakia, where Hana lived with her family, and later to Terezin and Auschwitz. As Ishioka learns about the original owner of the suitcase, she shares what she has learned with the children of Japan and with the brother of Hana Brady. (IT; SIR, SRBI; 4–12)

Misiroglu, G. (Ed.). (1999). *Imagine: The spirit of 20th-century American heroes*. New York: MJF Books.

This book contains black-and-white photographs and letters, speeches, or writings from 56 individuals considered to be American heroes. The book is formatted so that a photograph covers one page and the opposing page contains a sidebar of italicized information about the individual along with a primary-source document originated by the subject. Included are people such as Grandma Moses, Jim Henson, Louis Armstrong, Zora Neale Hurston, Sally Ride, and Bill Gates. (IT; SIR, SRBI; 4–12)

Rappaport, D. (2001). *Martin's big words: The life of Dr. Martin Luther King, Jr.* New York: Hyperion Books for Children.

Written by Doreen Rappaport and illustrated by Bryan Collier, this award-winning picture book is a biography of Dr. Martin Luther King, Jr. The book integrates text depicting events from King's life and statements made by King, as well as excerpts

---

The parenthetical information at the end of each annotation indicates the material's genre, the best use for the material, and appropriate grade range. *Genres*: N = novel, YA = young adult novel, PB = picture book, P = poetry, M = memoir, B = biography, SS = short story, IT = informational text. *Best Use*: TBI = teacher background information, TSRA = teacher and student read-aloud, SIR = student independent reading, SRBI = student research and background information.

from his speeches with collage illustrations created from paint, fabric, and print. (PB, B; TSRA, SRBI; 4–12)

Wallace, E., Vigness, D.M., & Ward, G.B. (2002). *Documents of Texas history* (2nd ed.). Austin: Texas State Historical Association.
> This book contains important documents that reflect Texas history, beginning with Cabeza de Vaca's shipwreck on the Texas coast in 1528 and concluding with events occurring in 1994. Sample documents include speeches, legal cases, newspaper reports, and book reviews. Each document is accompanied by an explanation and background information from the authors, who view the study of these documents as a way to begin to understand the history of Texas. (IT; SIR, SRBI; 8–12)

Wyman, R.M., Jr. (2005). *America's history through young voices: Using primary sources in the K–12 social studies classroom.* Upper Saddle River, NJ: Pearson Education.
> This work includes information on primary and secondary sources and descriptions of state standards and how primary sources might be used in the classroom. Letters, journals, diaries, essays, and some photographs for U.S. historical eras span from Colonial America to the Civil Rights era. (IT; TBI, TSRA, SIR, SRBI; 4–12)

Chapter 4
Discovering the Community: Reading Photographs to Write About Relevant Social Issues

Rylant, C. (1994). *Something permanent.* New York: Harcourt Brace.
> Photographs by Walker Evans taken during the U.S. Great Depression and poetry written by Cynthia Rylant are juxtaposed in this book. Because of the mature nature of some of the poems and/or photographs, teachers should preview the text and choose photographs and poems to share with the students. (P; TBI, TSRA; 4–12)

Stanley, J. (1992). *Children of the dust bowl: The true story of the school at Weedpatch Camp.* New York: Crown.
> This informational book, which includes black-and-white photographs, chronicles the movement from Oklahoma to migrant farm camps in California and the establishment of the Weedpatch School at one of the camps. (IT; TBI, TSRA, SIR, SRBI; 4–12)

Chapter 5
Envisioning People, Places, and Events: Reading Photographs to Write Narratives

Appelt, K. (2002). *Bubba and Beau, best friends.* San Diego, CA: Harcourt.
> Bubba, a young boy from Lubbock, Texas, is the son of Big Bubba and Mama Pearl. Beau, a hound pup, is the son of Maurice and Evelyn. In this picture book with

---

The parenthetical information at the end of each annotation indicates the material's genre, the best use for the material, and appropriate grade range. *Genres*: N = novel, YA = young adult novel, PB = picture book, P = poetry, M = memoir, B = biography, SS = short story, IT = informational text. *Best Use*: TBI = teacher background information, TSRA = teacher and student read-aloud, SIR = student independent reading, SRBI = student research and background information.

"chapters," Bubba and Beau become best friends and temporarily lose sight and scent of their beloved pink blankie. (PB; TSRA, SIR; 4–12)

Banyai, I. (1995). *Re-zoom*. New York: Puffin.
This second wordless book by Hungarian Istvan Banyai challenges readers' perceptions in the same manner as did *Zoom*. In *Re-Zoom*, we first see what appears to be an inkblot of an archer, which is really a figure printed on the face of a watch worn by a young man who is drawing. We move further and further into the images until we end up looking at the taillights on a subway car. (PB; TSRA, SIR; 4–12)

Banyai, I. (1995). *Zoom*. New York: Puffin.
This wordless text challenges readers' perceptions. As each new page is encountered, our understanding of what we are seeing and where we are in the world of the text is altered. We begin looking at what we think is the comb on a rooster's head and end with a view of earth as a dot in space. (PB; TSRA, SIR; 4–12)

Cisneros, S. (2002). *Caramelo*. New York: Knopf.
This book is a multigenerational story of a Mexican American family. We travel with the Reyes family on their annual car trip from Chicago to Mexico City. As we move back and forth in time, between Chicago; Mexico City; and San Antonio, Texas, we come to know the family history—sometimes real and sometimes not so real! Teachers could read aloud excerpts, or more mature readers could read on their own. (N, M; TSRA, SIR; 9–12)

Day, A. (1991). *Good dog, Carl*. New York: Simon & Schuster.
This wordless picture book features Carl the Rottweiler, who is left at home to babysit Madeleine. With Carl in charge, Madeleine bounces on the bed, plays dress up, swims in the aquarium, and has many more adventures before mom comes home. (PB; TSRA, SIR; 4–12)

Day, A. (1992). *Carl goes shopping*. New York: Farrar, Straus and Giroux.
In this wordless picture book, Carl the Rottweiler and Madeleine traverse the department store, sampling cookies and dog biscuits and looking at hats, toys, and books. When they see Madeleine's mother coming down the escalator, they rush to meet her at the baby carriage. (PB; TSRA, SIR; 4–12)

Day, A. (1992). *Carl's afternoon in the park*. New York: Farrar, Straus and Giroux.
When left in the park to babysit Madeleine, Carl the Rottweiler takes her and a new Rottweiler puppy on an adventure in which they ride a carousel, pose for painters, and play in the flowers in this wordless picture book. (PB; TSRA, SIR; 4–12)

Day, A. (1992). *Carl's Christmas*. New York: Farrar, Straus and Giroux.
In this wordless picture book, Carl the Rottweiler is left alone with Madeleine on Christmas Eve. They have a grand adventure in which they decorate a potted plant, sing with some carolers, encounter reindeer, and become "helpers" to Santa. (PB; TSRA, SIR; 4–12)

The parenthetical information at the end of each annotation indicates the material's genre, the best use for the material, and appropriate grade range. *Genres*: N = novel, YA = young adult novel, PB = picture book, P = poetry, M = memoir, B = biography, SS = short story, IT = informational text. *Best Use*: TBI = teacher background information, TSRA = teacher and student read-aloud, SIR = student independent reading, SRBI = student research and background information.

Day, A. (1995). *Carl goes to daycare*. New York: Farrar, Straus and Giroux.
In this wordless picture book, Carl the Rottweiler takes charge in the classroom at Madeleine's daycare when the teacher gets locked outside the door. (PB; TSRA, SIR; 4–12)

Day, A. (1997). *Carl's birthday*. New York: Farrar, Straus and Giroux.
In this wordless picture book, Carl the Rottweiler and Madeleine are sent next door while Madeleine's mother prepares a surprise birthday party for Carl. Carl and Madeleine sneak back to the house and, unseen by the mother, sample the birthday surprises. (PB; TSRA, SIR; 4–12)

Day, A. (2005). *Carl's sleepy afternoon*. New York: Farrar, Straus and Giroux.
In this wordless picture book, Carl the Rottweiler abandons his nap to travel across town to visit a bakery, to stop by a pharmacy, to help a veterinarian, to entertain children in the park, and to save a litter of puppies from a fire. (PB; TSRA, SIR; 4–12)

Hinton, S.E. (1967). *The outsiders*. New York: Dell.
This is the story of how two rival groups of teenagers with different ways of living and looking at life learn to accept one another. The Greasers and the Socials can be compared with current gangs. There is some violence, i.e., fighting and a stabbing, but there is a strong message about friendship and finding commonalities. (YA; TSRA, SIR; 7–12)

Wiesner, D. (1988). *Freefall*. New York: Scholastic.
In this wordless picture book, a young boy falls asleep and dreams of an adventure in a far-off land populated by living chess people, dragons, and giant books. While on his adventure, he is accompanied by a mysterious creature in a trench coat. (PB; TSRA, SIR; 4–12)

Wiesner, D. (1992). *June 29, 1999*. Boston: Houghton Mifflin.
This picture book with few words could be used as a wordless book by covering the text with sticky notes. Holly Evans plans to grow seedlings in airborne cartons. Shortly after the launch, giant-sized vegetables begin appearing all over the nation. Readers know that the vegetables come from an alien craft that has accidentally jettisoned its supply of food. Just as Holly wonders what has happened to her vegetable seedlings, we see them arrive at the spacecraft. (PB; TSRA, SIR; 4–12)

Wiesner, D. (2006). *Flotsam*. Boston: Houghton Mifflin.
In this wordless picture book, a curious-minded boy explores the beach, studying objects (or flotsam) that have washed ashore. When he finds a barnacle covered underwater camera and develops the film inside, we embark on a visual undersea adventure. (PB; TSRA, SIR; 4–12)

Note. Page numbers followed by *f* or *t* indicate figures or tables, respectively.

NARRATIVES, 126–152; based on art reproductions or book illustrations, 142–144; elements of, 133–137; partners for, 137–139; resources on, 162–164; sharing, 148–150, 148*f*–149*f*; two-voice, 140–142

NEW LITERACY CLASSROOMS: definition of, 13–14

NEW LONDON GROUP, 23–24

NEWMAN, A.L., 104

NODELMAN, P., 127

NOTEBOOK MUSEUM, 89

O

O'BRIEN, D., 6

OLIVER, M., 78

ORAL HISTORIES, 84–85; interviews, 89–93

P

PANETTA, E., 49, 57, 159

PARENTS: memoirs and, 42

PARTNERS: for narrative writing, 137–139

PERKINS, D.N., 42

PHOTO-BASED WRITING: biographies, 71–101; on community, 102–125; on identity, 44–70; instructional benefits of, 11–14; and literacy instruction, ix–xiii, 1–17; memoirs, 38–41, 40*f*; narratives, 126–152; understanding, 10–11

PHOTO COLLAGE: poems, 36–38; on scenes from literature, 56–58, 58*f*

PHOTOGRAPHS: of communities, 116–120, 117*f*–119*f*; as cultural and personal artifacts, 6; defining identity, essay on, 63–68, 65*f*, 68*f*; excerpts on, 35–36; and identity, texts on, 51–53; of interviewee, 90–92; and literacy instruction, ix–xiii, 1–17; meaningful conversations on, 22–25; for name

poems, 54–55, 55*f*; narratives based on, 144–150, 148*f*–149*f*; reading, meaning of, 6–8; on social issues, 105–109; sorting and categorizing, 20–22; student-generated, 24, 54; as texts, 3–6; value of, 2–3; writing about, 8–11

PHOTO-LIFE MAP, 59–62, 60*f*, 62*f*

PHOTO MUSEUMS, 22–25

PICTURE BOOKS: on memoirs, 21*t*, 25–28; on narrative elements, 134

POEMS: biographical, 78–80, 80*f*; Found, 109–112; Important, 81–83; on names, 53–56; photo collage, 36–38

POLACCO, P., 51, 158

POPULAR CULTURE: and literacy instruction, 104

POSTCARDS: voice in, 86–88

PRIMARY-SOURCE DOCUMENTS, 83–89; published, 84

PROMPTS: for narrative writing, 138–139

PROSE POEMS: biographical, 78–80, 80*f*; definition of, 78–79

R

RAPPAPORT, D., 74, 83, 94–95, 160

RANKIN-ERICKSON, J.L., 11

READERS THEATRE, 48

READING: community, 112–115; photographs, meaning of, 6–8; resources for, 153–164; shared, 47–48

REFLECTION POINTS: on advertisements, 133; on biographies, 78, 96; on book club, 51; on creative opportunities, 83; on demonstrating writing process, 67; on discussion, 120; on excerpts, 36; on expectations, 123; on found poems, 112; on identity, 55–56, 58; on journals, 89; on list memoirs, 34–35; on memoirs, 28, 31–32, 41; on narratives, 130, 142;

on observation, 148; on oral history, 86, 93; on Photo-Life Map, 62; on photo museums, 25; on picture books, 137; on prompts, 139; on "remember" photo collage poems, 38; on social issues, 115; on sorting and categorizing photographs, 22; on texts connecting photos and identity, 53; on visual analysis, 108; on voice, 75; on websites, 80

"REMEMBER" PHOTO COLLAGE POEMS, 36–38

RINGGOLD, F., 27, 156

ROCHMAN, H., 49, 159

ROMANO, T., 78

RYLANT, C., 107, 161

S

SAROYAN, WILLIAM, 16

SCENES: defining, 56; from literature, photo collage on, 56–58, 58f

SCHMITZER, J.C., 77, 159

SCIENCE: photo-based literacy instruction in, 15

SEEING: aspects of, 8

SHARED READING, 47–48

SHORT STORIES: on identity, 49, 51

SHREVE, A., 150

SIMPSON, A., 73

SMITH, CLYDE "KINGFISH", 85

SOCIAL INTERACTION: and literacy, 23

SOCIAL ISSUES: excerpts on, 109–112; journal entries on, 112–115; photographs on, 105–109; resources on, 106t, 112t, 161–162; selection of, 120–123, 121f–122f; writing about, 102–125

SOCIAL STUDIES: photo-based literacy instruction in, 14–15

SOLOMON, B.H., 49, 57, 159

SONTAG, SUSAN, 8

SOTO, G., 49, 159

STANLEY, J., 110, 161

STANLEY, N., 46

STEIN, P., 73

STORIES. See narratives; short stories

STORYCORPS, 84–85

STURKEN, M., 7

T

TAULBERT, C.L., 28, 156

TAYLOR, E.W., 45

TEGANO, D.W., 4, 7

TEXTS: definition of, 3; photographs as, 3–6; selection of, resources for, 153–164. See also visual texts

TWO-VOICE NARRATIVES, 140–142

U–V

URDANIVIA-ENGLISH, C., 46

VAN HORN, L., ix, 49

VAN SLUYS, K., 72

VIGNESS, D.M., 84, 161

VISUAL TEXTS, 3–4; analysis of, 108–109; literacy with, 127–128; and written communication, 5–6. See also texts

VOICE: in biographies, 71–101; concept of, introducing, 74–75; importance of, 83–89; in journals, 83, 88–89; in narratives, 142; in postcards, 86–88

W–Z

WALKER, R., 49, 57, 159

WALLACE, E., 84, 161

WARD, G.B., 84, 161

WATTS, J.H., 25, 156

WEBSITES, 80; on memoirs, 30t; of social issues photographs, 106

WELTY, E., 19

WESTCOTT, W., 127

WIESNER, D., 135, 163

WINK, J., 13

WOLFF, T., 28, 156

WOOD, G.S., 99

WOOTON, K., 104